Springer Series on Cultural Computing

Cultural Computing is an exciting, emerging field of Human Computer Interaction, which covers the cultural impact of computing and the technological influences and requirements for the support of cultural innovation. Using support technologies such as artificial intelligence, machine learning, location-based systems, mixed/virtual/augmented reality, cloud computing, pervasive technologies and human-data interaction, researchers can explore the differences across a variety of cultures and cultural production to provide the knowledge and skills necessary to overcome cultural issues and expand human creativity.

This series presents monographs, edited collections and advanced textbooks on the current research and knowledge of a broad range of topics including creativity support systems, creative computing, digital communities, the interactive arts, cultural heritage, digital culture and intercultural collaboration.

This Series is abstracted/indexed in Scopus.

Francesca Franco

The Algorithmic Dimension

Five Artists in Conversation

 Springer

Francesca Franco
College of Humanities
University of Exeter
Devon, UK

ISSN 2195-9056   ISSN 2195-9064 (electronic)
Springer Series on Cultural Computing
ISBN 978-3-031-13386-2   ISBN 978-3-319-61167-9 (eBook)
https://doi.org/10.1007/978-3-319-61167-9

This Springer imprint is published by the registered company Springer Nature Switzerland AG
The registered company address is: Gewerbestrasse 11, 6330 Cham, Switzerland

To Vera, Ernest, Manfred, Frieder and Roman

Acknowledgements

I am most indebted to Ernest Edmonds, Manfred Mohr, Vera Molnár, Frieder Nake and Roman Verostko, who have inspired my research in the history of pioneering computational art and kindly accepted my invitation to take part in the various events documented in this book. The privilege of having been able to spend so much precious time sharing thoughts, laughs and life stories with them was for me a cherished and humbling experience. Curating an exhibition focussed on their work and bringing their art to my own hometown against one of the most beautiful backdrops one could ever imagine was an even greater dream come true. For these reasons, and on account of the personal affection I feel for these incredibly brave and profound artists, I dedicate this book to them.

I would like to express my gratitude to the Fondazione Bevilacqua La Masa and the *Comune di Venezia*, in particular Michele Casarin, Bruno Bernardi and Stefano Coletto, for giving me the opportunity to work with them and for hosting and producing *Algorithmic Signs*. I am particularly indebted to Stefano Coletto for his sincere guidance, the time and effort he dedicated to the production of the exhibition, and the curatorial expertise he so generously shared with me. His insights into every step of the curatorial process gave me an invaluable lesson that I will treasure. I would like to extend my gratitude to the entire staff of the Fondazione Bevilacqua La Masa for their help during the various stages in the setting up of the exhibition, in particular Enrica Sbrogiò and Claudio Donadel for their support and cheerful cama-raderie that made some of the most challenging stages of the exhibition organisation much lighter and more joyful.

I am extremely grateful to Anne and Michael Spalter for their generosity in lending key and rare works from their extraordinary Digital Art Collection. Without their support and patronage the exhibition would not have been complete. I would also like to extend my gratitude to Douglas Dodds, at the Victoria and Albert Museum, who has been instrumental in facilitating the lending of a number of works for the exhibition and kindly helped by making research material available.

Special thanks are due to those who gave their time to read or edit my manuscript or parts of it, including Sandra Denby and Sylvia Hochfield. I would also like to thank Vincent Baby, Claudia Hermes, Florent Paumelle and Keiko Yoshida for their precious help during the final stages of my writing. I am particularly grateful to Steven Holt for his meticulous copyediting skills and the care and accuracy of his work.

For providing the images, I would like to thank the artists, Anne and Michael Spalter, the Victoria and Albert Museum, and GV Art London. Special thanks are due to the photographers Giorgio Bombieri, Thales Leite, Jules Lister and Pier Parimbelli, who kindly granted permission to publish their images. I also thank CamuffoLab in Venice and everyone who contributed to designing the exhibition's poster from an original idea of Stefano Coletto and with the valuable advice of David Bates, Sean Clark, Piero Cornice, Christian Harris and Thomas Pircher.

I am most grateful to my editor Helen Desmond at Springer for her helpful support and assistance. A big thank you goes to Michela Castrica for her support during the final stages of publication, and to everyone at Springer for their editorial support.

Finally, and most importantly, I wish to thank my parents for their love and constant encouragement over the years, and my husband for his love, patience and the many conversations we have that give me new perspectives and inspiration that enrich my life.

Contents

Chapter 1
Introduction

This book examines *Algorithmic Signs*, an exhibition conceived, researched and curated by the author. The exhibition was held at the Fondazione Bevilacqua La Masa's historical gallery in St Mark's Square, Venice, from 19 October until 3 December 2017. The book also aims at documenting the author's research on the history of computational art at the core of *Algorithmic Signs* that developed out of a series of meetings, collectively named *The Algorithmic Dimension*, that she co-organised and led in Leicester and Sheffield in 2012. They included an all-day event celebrating early computer art with international pioneers in the world of digital arts, Ernest Edmonds, Manfred Mohr, Frieder Nake and Roman Verostko discussing the role of programming in their art with the author, Douglas Dodds, Leila Johnston, Alex May, Richard Sides and Laura Sillars in Sheffield on 17 November; and the *Algorithmic Dimension* masterclass, an event organised and chaired by the author in partnership with De Montfort University and Phoenix, Leicester, on 19 November 2012, where Edmonds, Nake and Verostko explored the role of programming in their work, looking at how their practice has kept pace with the rapid advance of technology in recent decades. This was followed by a series of artist interviews conducted in London, Paris, Bremen, Venice and New York over the past six years. The research morphed into *Algorithmic Signs*, a curatorial project that began to take shape on a foggy afternoon in Venice in December 2015 and became a reality in October 2017 at the Fondazione Bevilacqua La Masa, one of the most ancient and respected institutions devoted to supporting the development of contemporary art in Venice. This exhibition explored the history of pioneering computational art and its contribution to the broader field of contemporary art from the 1960s to the present. The history was exemplified by the creative work of Ernest Edmonds, Manfred Mohr, Vera Molnár, Frieder Nake and Roman Verostko. The author presents the historical context and main concepts that led to the creation of this exhibition. In addition, the author demonstrates how *Algorithmic Signs* provided new interpretations of the history of computer art.

© Springer Nature Switzerland AG 2022
F. Franco, *The Algorithmic Dimension*, Springer Series on Cultural Computing,
https://doi.org/10.1007/978-3-319-61167-9_1

1.1   Background

Given what we know about the influence of Venetian art on the arts, particularly from the Byzantine period to the Renaissance and up to the eighteenth century, Venice and algorithmic art are not the most obvious association in the art world.

Finding computational art in Venice therefore represents a new, fascinating and exciting adventure. It is an even more challenging task due to its hybrid, fluid nature, and because this art (using the computer as a tool or medium), although in existence since the mid-1950s, has not been fully accepted by the traditional art institutions and has been overlooked for many years. Despite the fact that major exhibitions on art and technology have been shown internationally from the late 1960s to the early 1970s, the sense of excitement instilled by these exhibitions was short-lived, and exhibitions on computer art have been a rarity during the past fifty years.

Personally, I have been involved in this search since I started my postgraduate studies in London more than fifteen years ago. It became the focus of my PhD thesis and, since finishing my doctorate, as an art historian researching the connections between art and technology, it still remains a constant interest of mine. There is a more personal reason why I find this search fascinating, namely I was born in Venice and studied fine art and art history there. The idea of bringing some of the most influential pioneers of algorithmic art, whose work has been the focus of my research for the past decade, to my birthplace represents a "coming home" that recalls memories both of my childhood and of my student life, which were distinctively filled with a passion for contemporary art.

Contemporary art in Venice has had a relatively long history that dates back to the first Venice Biennale in 1895 (Franco 2012). But, as English art historian and curator Lawrence Alloway extensively demonstrated in his *The Venice Biennale, 1895–1968: From Salon to Goldfish Bowl* (Alloway 1968), the first Biennales, particularly between 1895 and 1914, were devoted to the celebration of the official academic style, or "Salon art". Far from being innovative and open to the new European tendencies, the first Biennales demonstrated a conservative and reassuring attitude towards art. The breaking apart of the Venice Biennale's original curatorial model occurred due to political circumstances in 1968, the year of European radical revolts for social and economic change. From a curatorial point of view, the 1968 Venice Biennale represented an "anomaly" in comparison with its previous renditions. Not only the political demands brought forward by the student revolt, but also the introduction of new technologies in art from the mid-1960s contributed stimulation and allowed the Venice Biennale to distance itself from its original nineteenth-century Salon art model. Owing to innovative and cross-disciplinary projects such as those presented by Argentinian artist David Lamelas and French cybernetic artist Nicolas Schöffer at the 1968 Biennale, the institution started, slowly, to open up towards new media and to accept them as a new form of art.

The 1970 Biennale represented a fundamental step for the art institution in the long journey towards the acceptance of computer art (Franco 2013). The Biennale's major show *Ricerca e Progettazione. Proposte per una Esposizione Sperimentale (Research and Planning. Proposals for an Experimental Exhibition*) was curated by Umbro Apollonio and Dietrich Mahlow. It was an exhibition entirely devoted to "experimental art" and included a large selection of early computer art arranged historically and thematically. The artworks using computer-generated programs included "Return to a Square" by the Computer Technique Group, "Electronic Graphics" by Herbert W. Franke, works by Auro Lecci, "Matrix Multiplication" by Frieder Nake (brought back to Venice for the first time for *Algorithmic Signs*), "Computer Graphics" by Georg Nees and a computer-generated sculpture by Richard C. Raymond. The 1970 show was experimental. It was an anomaly, not a tradition, and it demonstrated—for the first time in Venice—that computer art could be seen as a way to find a vital function, or a purpose, of art in society.

The mid-1980s witnessed the first genuine attempt at a historicisation of computer art. A seminal example was given by the major retrospective of computer art organised by American art historian Patric Prince for SIGGRAPH in 1986. The historicisation of computer art in the mid-1980s can be seen as an essential factor that helped make computer art "safe". It allowed the acceptance of computational art material in conservative art institutions worldwide, particularly the Venice Biennale. The opening up of the Biennale towards art and technology in the 1980s—anticipated by the 1970 Biennale's *Proposte per una Esposizione Sperimentale*—started very timidly in 1980 with a peripheral show, *Cronografie*, curated by historian Gianfranco Bettettini for the 1980 Venice Biennale's side event *Il Tempo dell'Uomo nella Società della Tecnica*. The show was exclusively dedicated to the role of memory and time in contemporary society, with a focus on new technologies.

The openness of the Biennale towards art and technology unfolded more rapidly in the mid-1980s, particularly with the 1986 thematic edition on *Art and Science* directed by art historian Maurizio Calvesi. *Technology and Informatics* was the most cutting-edge project presented there, and it took place in the restored Corderie dell'Arsenale. One of the most inspiring projects exhibited there was *Networking*, a show curated by Roy Ascott, Don Foresta, Tom Sherman and Tommaso Trini. *Networking* included interactive installations by Waltraut Cooper, Brian Eno, Piero Fogliati, Liliane Lijn, Maurizio Mochetti, David Rokeby and Bill Viola; a "laboratory-workshop" that presented videotext artworks selected by Red Burns from New York University; a small section on laser disc creations; a "computer imaging" section including computer-generated artworks by Adriano Abbado, Olivier Agid, Roberto Matta and Anne-Marie Pécheur; and a personal contribution by Ascott, "Planetary Network", a project co-authored with Robert Adrian that explored the notion of telematic interactivity.

In the 1990s, art and technology—particularly video art—became openly accepted, exhibited and eventually awarded prizes. In 1990, for instance, American artist Jenny Holzer received the Biennale's Best Pavilion Award and in 1993, Korean-born American video artist Nam June Paik was awarded the same prestigious award, ex-aequo with Hans Haacke, for his video installation "Sistine Chapel". In 1999, Doug Aitken won the Golden Lion with his video installation "Electric Earth".

Apart from the rare exception represented by the 1970 Biennale's experimental show, computer art at the Biennale has since been exhibited only peripherally. And it seems that, even today, most of the cutting-edge projects are exhibited outside the official site of the Giardini.

Algorithmic Signs represents the first attempt after the 1970 Biennale to bring early computational art and some of its most prominent pioneers back to Venice (Figs. 1.1 and 1.2). It explores the history of pioneering generative art and its contribution to the broader field of contemporary art from the 1960s to the present. The artists who pioneered this work are sometimes known as the "Algorists". The history is exemplified in the creative work of five international pioneers in the world of digital arts: Ernest Edmonds (b. 1942), Manfred Mohr (b. 1938), Vera Molnar (b. 1924), Frieder Nake (b. 1938) and Roman Verostko (b. 1929). Coming to the computer from completely different backgrounds and experiences—monastic life, jazz music, traditional painting, philosophy, mathematics and studies of logic—they began to experiment with the creative use of the algorithm and computer code to construct their works and make art.

Fifty years after the first experiments in computational art, international interest in the history of this subject remains strong, despite the comparative paucity of exhibitions and published studies. This exhibition is the first to describe one of the possible histories of this almost unexplored but extremely dynamic field of contemporary art, from the perspective of some of its most celebrated pioneers. Focussing on the relationship between computer programming, art and creativity, the presentation of each artist explores the role of programming in their work, looking at how their practice has kept pace with the rapid advance of technology in recent decades.

Fig. 1.1 "Algorithmic Signs" poster. ©Fondazione Bevilacqua La Masa. Image courtesy of Fondazione Bevilacqua La Masa

```
C:\Algorithmic Signs>
.
..
>Ernest Edmonds
>Manfred Mohr
>Vera Molnár
>Frieder Nake
>Roman Verostko


Istituzione Fondazione/
Bevilacqua La Masa

Galleria di Piazza
San Marco/Venezia

19.10_03.12.2017
```

Fig. 1.2 Entrance of Fondazione Bevilacqua La Masa, galleria di Piazza San Marco. ©Francesca Franco

1.2 Algorithmic Signs

Algorithmic Signs offers the viewer the rare opportunity to see the histories and developments of the fascinating art created though the algorithm in an accessible and stimulating narrative, and looks closely at the role of coding in contemporary art practice. The exhibition follows the personal achievements of each artist, their original inspirations, and how they developed in parallel with technological advances. It also brings together for the first time ever the artists' common ideas and differences, and tells about how their paths have crossed over the years.

Through a rigorous and astonishingly consistent practice, the five artists represented in *Algorithmic Signs* demonstrate how their creativity has been enhanced and amplified with the aid of the machine through the creative use of the algorithm.

Ernest Edmonds' art explores colour, time and interaction in the context of colour field painting and systems art. His work extends the Constructivist tradition into the digital age in a powerful and enduring investigation of mathematical and computational systems (Franco 2017). Some of the major artworks that define Edmonds' singular achievement are exhibited in this show.

They include early generative computer-based art systems, such as "Nagoya" (1996) (Fig. 1.3), and his most recent works in which the artist has explored the potential of an interactive audience in public spaces, extending interactivity to a more comprehensive new form of collective behaviour, and has extended the notion of interactive art to include long-term influence, as in works such as the "Shaping Form" series (from 2007) and "Shaping Space" (2012) (Fig. 1.4).

"Shaping Form" consists of a series of works on individual stand-alone screens framed so that the image is square (Fig. 1.5). The early frames were in white acrylic (Fig. 1.6). Movement in front of each work is detected by a small camera. This leads to continual changes in the program that generates the images. A viewer can readily detect the immediate responses of the work to movement but, as Edmonds points out, "the changes over time are only apparent when there is more prolonged, although not necessarily continuous, contact with it. A first viewing followed by one several months later will reveal noticeable developments in the colours and patterns." The crucial innovation that this new line of work brought to Edmonds' art was the move from simple interaction to what he terms "influence":

> By recording and analysing the interactions, the software 'learns' from experience about human reaction to the artwork. The Video Construct changes its behaviour in the light of its experience with human participants interacting with the work. [...] we can consider the

Fig. 1.3 Ernest Edmonds, *Nagoya*, 1996. ©Ernest Edmonds. Image courtesy of the artist

Fig. 1.4 Ernest Edmonds, *Shaping Space*—installation at Site Gallery, Sheffield, 2012. ©Francesca Franco

artwork and the audience as interacting systems that influence one another. We can consider the development of Computational art systems that are open to influence and that develop over time as a consequence. (Edmonds and Muller 2005, p. 305)

Manfred Mohr is a pioneer of computer-generated algorithmic art. After his discovery of Max Bense's *Information Aesthetics* in the early 1960s, Mohr's art transformed from abstract expressionism to computer-generated geometric art. Mohr programmed his first computer drawings in 1969. In 1971, Mohr had the first one-person show of digital computer-generated art in a museum, at the Musée d'Art Moderne de la Ville de Paris, France (Fig. 1.7).

In 1969, the introduction into his art of the computer together with a mechanical drawing device, the plotter, extended Mohr's creativity and helped him create signs generated by the rational structure of programming and algorithmic processes (Figs. 1.8 and 1.9).

As he stated in 1985,

I call my work 'generative' because all my work is generated from algorithms (logical processes) worked out by myself beforehand. This is my fundamental contribution to aesthetic research. I create signs, graphic existences, out of rational context. These signs refer only to themselves and their content is evidence of their creation. A logical and straightforward development of my work was the introduction of a computer and of a plotter in 1969. Dialogue with the machine thus became an important part of my work – an irreversible extension and/or amplification of my artistic thought. (Mohr 1985)

This led to a new phase in Mohr's art, whereby a logical and automatic construction of pictures was introduced into his work. For the first time in his art, algorithms were used to calculate the images. The resulting drawings were made by a computer-controlled drawing machine (plotter). So, for example, in works such as "P-021"

Fig. 1.5 Ernest Edmonds,
Shaping Form, 1.5.2015,
2015. ©Ernest Edmonds.
Photograph courtesy of
Thales Leite

(1969) (Fig. 1.10) with a choice of different line characteristics, such as horizontal elements, vertical lines and zigzags that move mostly from left to right, an abstract text was created. It is basically an alphabet of arbitrarily generated elements.

From 1972, Manfred began employing the structure of the cube as a system and alphabet (Fig. 1.11), and, as the works exhibited in *Algorithmic Signs* demonstrate, over the years he will always maintain the structural elements and constraints of the cube in his vocabulary.

Vera Molnar is one of the pioneers of computer and algorithmic arts. Born in Hungary in 1924, Molnar initially trained as a traditional artist, studying fine arts and obtaining a diploma in art history and aesthetics from the Budapest College of Fine Arts. Inspired by abstract, geometrically and systematically determined painting, she created her first abstract works in 1946. After receiving an artist's fellowship at the Villa Giulia, Rome, she moved to France, where she still lives and works. In 1968, she began working with computers, and started to create algorithmic paintings based on simple geometric shapes and themes. One of her most moving works, "Lettres à ma mère", is exhibited for the first time here in Venice. It is a series of works Molnar

Fig. 1.6 Ernest Edmonds, *Shaping Form*, 2007. ©Ernest Edmonds. Image courtesy of the prints, drawings and paintings collection, the Victoria and Albert Museum, London

created between 1981 and 1990 with the aid of a computer and a plotter to recreate the handwriting of her mother (Figs. 1.12, 1.13 and 1.14).

As Molnar recalls,

My mother had beautiful handwriting – somewhat Gothic, somewhat hysterical. She began each line regularly and strictly with Gothic letters, which toward the end of the line became more and more restless, nervous, almost hysterical. As she aged, the letters became quite troubled, perturbed. Slowly the Gothic disappeared, leaving only the hysterical. The colour of the writing transformed, too. At the beginning of our correspondence, she used a light blue ink, the colour of her eyes. Over the years, this blue gradually turned into black. Each week I received a letter, which meant a real experience for my visual world. The letters were more and more difficult to decipher but they looked very pleasant. After her death, there were no more letters … I started 'simulating' on computer her gothical-hysterical missives to myself. (Molnar 1995, p. 167)

Satisfied by the visual qualities of these works, Molnar describes the creative process behind them thus:

The visual aspect in these pieces, executed with computer and plotter, changes evenly at every line, proceeding from left to right. Using an increasingly random process, the lines – built up with regular sequences going up and down with a tilt of 110–120 degrees – become more and more chaotic as they advance to the right. This phenomenon occurs within each line, within each letter. The letters become more and more disturbed. The relative order seen in the first letters, on the left side, disappears progressively. This is a hair-raising solution for a painter like myself with a classical education. There is no symmetry, no equilibrium, no transversal, no triangle. Would the whole thing be held together by the fact that it is the simulation of writing, that it is my mother's writing? But this is not one of the principles of the visual arts. This I immediately understood. I tried various ways to reconcile and bring together the two different and opposing areas: visual arts and my mother's dishevelled writing. Though

Fig. 1.7 Poster of Manfred Mohr's one-person show, May 11–June 6, 1971, Musée d'Art Moderne de la Ville de Paris, France. ©Manfred Mohr. Image courtesy of the artist

Fig. 1.8 Manfred Mohr changing plotter pens at the Institut Météorologique, Paris 1970. ©Manfred Mohr. Image courtesy of the artist

Fig. 1.9 Manfred Mohr checking the computer controlled plotter at the Institut Météorologique, Paris 1970. ©Manfred Mohr. Image courtesy of the artist

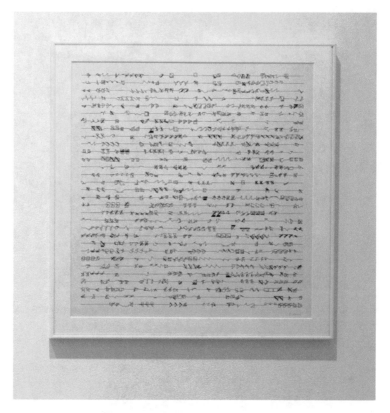

Fig. 1.10 Manfred Mohr, *P-021*, 1969. ©Manfred Mohr. Image courtesy of the artist

the whole thing is against the rules, in practice I am pleased with the result! (Molnar 1995, p. 169)

Frieder Nake is one of the founding fathers of computer art. He studied mathematics and, "by accident" (as he likes to say), in 1963, became a pioneer of algorithmic art. He had his first exhibition in November 1965 (Galerie Wendelin Niedlich, Stuttgart). He has participated in all of the major international exhibitions on computational art, including *Tendencies 4* (Zagreb 1968), *Cybernetic Serendipity* (London 1968) and the first computer art show at the Venice Biennale in 1970 (Franco 2013), among others. In 1970, he made a poignant announcement through the Computer Art Society's bulletin PAGE. Here Nake stated that he was going to stop exhibiting, the main reason being the fact that computer art was becoming too commercial:

I stop exhibiting for the present (last exhibition, in form of a retrospective, with H. de Vries at Swart Gallery, Amsterdam). Reason: it looks as if the capitalist art market is trying to get hold of computer productions. This would mean a distraction from visual research. Exhibiting in universities etc. is different as it helps to communicate; communication is essential to research. The actual production in artistic computer graphics is repeating itself to a great extent. Really good ideas haven't shown up for quite a while. (Nake 1971, n.p.)

Fig. 1.11 Manfred Mohr, *P-1273_3070*, 2007. ©Manfred Mohr. Image courtesy of the artist

This statement was followed by a paper entitled "There Should Be No Computer Art" presented by Nake during the International Colloquium on Arts and Computers in Zagreb in June 1971 (which was attended by a delegation from the Venice Biennale, among many others).

"There should be no computer art." Ethically, he felt, this was necessary. In the mid-1980s he slowly returned to the field of computational art. Over the last thirty years, he has exhibited and lectured around the world, and published his work in various academic publications. Recent exhibitions include *Frieder Nake* (Kunsthalle Bremen, 2004), *Imaging by Numbers* (Mary & Leigh Block Museum of Art Chicago, 2008), *No message whatsoever* (DAM, Berlin 2013–2014), *Primary Codes* (Oi Futuro, Rio de Janeiro, 2015), *Electronic Superhighway* (Whitechapel Gallery London, 2016), *Kunst in Europa 1945–1968* (ZKM Karlsruhe, 2016–2017). His work is represented at the Kunsthalle Bremen, the Tate Modern, London, The Anne and Michael Spalter Collection, the Sprengel Museum Hannover, the Victoria & Albert Museum, London, and the Museum of Contemporary Art Zagreb.

"Matrix Multiplication" (Fig. 1.15), back in Venice for the first time since it was exhibited at the 1970 Biennale, is one of the most iconic computer-generated artworks, and one of the earliest examples of full-colour continuous drawings generated by a computer.

Fig. 1.12 Vera Molnar, *Lettres à ma mere*, 1981–1990. ©Vera Molnar. Image courtesy of the Anne and Michael Digital Art Collection

Consisting of a grid of little squares where colours have been assigned by mathematical process, the work presents a series of variations that, as Frank Dietrich described in 1986, "reflect the translation of a mathematical process into an aesthetic process". He goes on to note that

> A square matrix was initially filled with numbers. The matrix was multiplied successively by itself, and the resulting new matrices were translated into images of predetermined intervals. Each number was assigned a visual sign with a particular form and colour. These signs were placed in a raster according to the numeric values of the matrix. The images were computed on an AEG/Telefunken TR4 programmed in ALGOL 60 and were plotted with a ZUSE Graphomat Z64. (Dietrich 1986, p. 161)

Roman Verostko is best known for his richly coloured algorithmic pen and brush drawings. Born in 1929 in the USA, he was schooled as an artist at the Art Institute of Pittsburgh (Diploma, 1949). A year later he entered monastic life at St Vincent Arch abbey in Latrobe, Pennsylvania, where he became deeply involved with art and spirituality. Following studies in Philosophy (BA, 1955) and theology (Ordination,

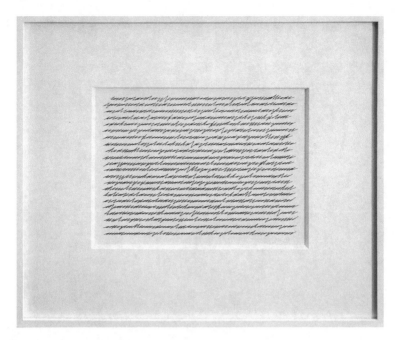

Fig. 1.13 Vera Molnar, *Lettres à ma mere*, 1981–1990. ©Vera Molnar. Image courtesy of the Anne and Michael Digital Art Collection

1959) he was sent to New York and Paris to pursue further studies both in studio practice (Pratt Institute, MFA) and in art history (Columbia and NYU); in Paris, he worked with Stanley William Hayter at Atelier 17 (1962–1963) and maintained a studio where he experimented with automatism and expressionist brushwork.

After having returned to the monastery, he developed his "New City" paintings and began experimenting with electronically synchronised audiovisuals. Roman departed from monastic life in 1968, married Alice Wagstaff, and joined the humanities faculty of the Minneapolis College of Art & Design in Minnesota. Roman's work with electronic synchronisers led him to an interest in computer circuits and programming. He followed a night course in FORTRAN at the Control Data Institute in 1970, gained more experience with circuits, and continued painting and programming electronic audio-visuals. He had access to an Apple at MCAD in 1978, acquired a studio PC in 1981, and coded a series of visual sequences that he exhibited in 1982 as "The Magic Hand of Chance" (Figs. 1.16, 1.17, 1.18 and 1.19). This program, written in BASIC, grew into his master drawing program, Hodos, generating his art-form ideas with both ink pens and brushes mounted on drawing machines. The front and end pieces for his 1990 limited edition "George Boole's 'Derivation of the Laws ...'" demonstrated the emerging power of generative art.

Notable among his projects are those he created to honour three pioneers whose work contributed to the information revolution of the last half of the twentieth century: George Boole, for his work with the Laws of Thought; Alan Turing, for his work

Fig. 1.14 Vera Molnar, *Lettres à ma mere*, 1981–1990. ©Vera Molnar. Image courtesy of the Anne and Michael Digital Art Collection

on Computable Numbers; and Norbert Wiener, for his work on cybernetics and the human control of machines.

Algorithmic Signs presents some of Verostko's most celebrated algorithmic poetry drawings. Among them, "Green Cloud" belongs to a recent series that was exhibited as a form of "visual poetry". To succeed, algorithms must adhere to a rigid syntax and the unforgiving demands of logical precision. The visual form of this drawing speaks eloquently of the grace and beauty that can be generated from the severely stark logic of disciplined code. A video documentation of the entire drawing procedure, "Three Story Drawing Machine" (2011), is shown at *Algorithmic Signs* (Fig. 1.20). The video shows the machine's drawing arm moving vertically on the three-storey wall for approximately eight hours, from the first stroke to the last. As dawn approached, a brush was mounted on the drawing arm and it proceeded to execute twelve calligraphic brush strokes completing the visual poetry.

As part of *Algorithmic Signs*, Verostko has created a new artwork, the "San Marco Apocalypse: Lifting the Veil" (2017), which is stylistically inspired by his early visual poetry works (Fig. 1.21).

Talking about the "San Marco Apocalypse", he states that

The term Apocalypse refers to an unveiling of something hidden or unknown, a revelation. This work illuminates a text coded in a glyphic format. When I first read this passage from Lao-Tzu, I experienced it as a 'lifting of the veil', a revelation that gave me insight into my struggle with the 'resolution of opposites'. (Verostko 2017)

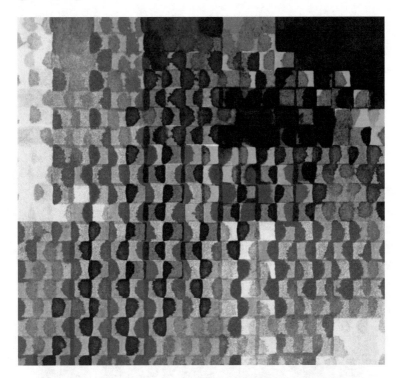

Fig. 1.15 Frieder Nake, *Matrix Multiplication series 39* (detail), 1968. ©Frieder Nake. Image courtesy of the artist

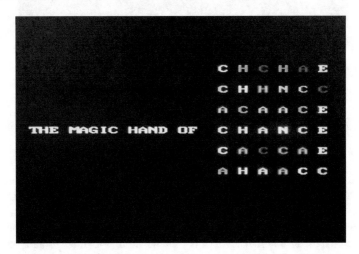

Fig. 1.16 Roman Verostko, *The Magic Hand of Chance*, 1982–84 (still image from a sequence). ©Roman Verostko. Image courtesy of the artist

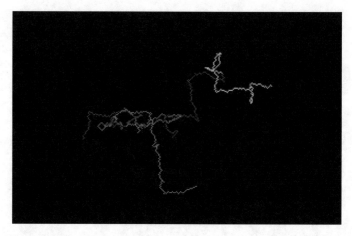

Fig. 1.17 Roman Verostko, *The Magic Hand of Chance*, 1982–84 (still image from a sequence). ©Roman Verostko. Image courtesy of the artist

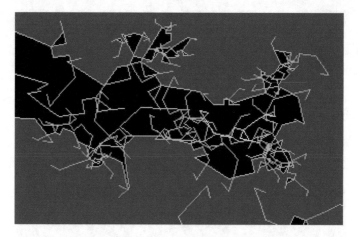

Fig. 1.18 Roman Verostko, *The Magic Hand of Chance*, 1982–84 (still image from a sequence). ©Roman Verostko. Image courtesy of the artist

One of the challenges of this exhibition was to open up new perspectives and uncover a new level of understanding of the intricacies of media art, to reveal aspects of creativity that have helped shape its complex history. The works on display demonstrate how human thought could be amplified by machines and could raise our consciousness to a higher level of comprehension, both intellectually and visually. With their rational methods, these artists have enabled a fuller understanding of the creative process.

By capturing the spirit of the time when the first experiments in computational art took place, and by looking at the developments of computer programming in art

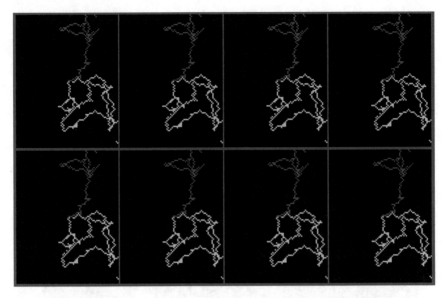

Fig. 1.19 Roman Verostko, *The Magic Hand of Chance*, 1982–84 (still image from a sequence). ©Roman Verostko. Image courtesy of the artist

Fig. 1.20 Roman Verostko, *Three Story Drawing Machine*, 2011. ©Roman Verostko. Image courtesy of the artist

up to the present time, *Algorithmic Signs* also reveals an often overlooked link that connects the work of the five exhibiting artists to past artistic traditions. In particular, the carefully structured and organised works in *Algorithmic Signs* demonstrate unequivocal affinities with the tradition of Constructivism, the modern art movement that began in Russia in the early twentieth century. Being based on the supremacy of the functionality of the art object over its exterior appearance and composition,

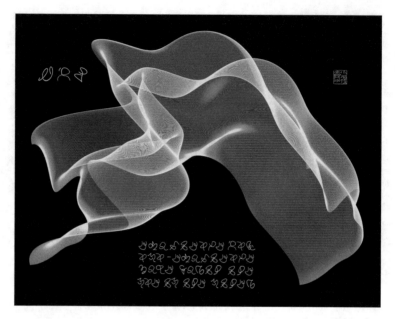

Fig. 1.21 Roman Verostko, *San Marco Apocalypse: Lifting the Veil*, 2017. ©Roman Verostko. Image courtesy of the artist

Constructivism inspired artists to explore the potential of modern materials and their role in expressing a new dynamism in modern life. Similarly to the way Vladimir Tatlin, one of the founding figures of Constructivism, explored the potential of new materials in his creations, Edmonds, Mohr, Molnar, Nake and Verostko have investigated the materiality of the art object and its organising structures in the context of computing technologies. With their rational methods, these artists have also enabled a fuller understanding of the creative process. They represent the missing fragment of the mosaic that connects this multifaceted and sophisticated line of research and that links the past and future of media art.

Algorithmic Signs aims at sparking a much-needed dialogue about the role of computation in contemporary art. This dialogue would allow computational art to be acknowledged not only as a dynamic and creative form of art that represents an essential part of art historiography but also as a dynamic field of research that is still alive and has been made tangible by its artists.

References

Alloway, Lawrence (1968). *The Venice Biennale, 1895–1968: From Salon to Goldfish Bowl* (Greenwich, Conn.: New York Graphic Society).

Dietrich, Frank (1986). "Visual Intelligence: The First Decade of Computer Art (1965–1975)", *Leonardo*, Vol. 19, No. 2, pp. 159–169.

Edmonds, Ernest, and Muller, Lizzie (2005). "On Creative Engagement", in *Computational and Cognitive Models of Creative Design VI*, Gero, John Steven, and Maher, Mary Lou (Eds.) (Sidney: Key Centre of Design Computing and Cognition, University of Sydney), pp. 303–318.

Franco, Francesca (2012). "Ars Ex Machina – The Missing History of New Media Art at the Venice Biennale, 1966–1986" (Ph.D. diss., School of History of Art, Film and Visual Media, Birkbeck University of London).

Franco, Francesca (2013). "The First Computer Art Show at the 1970 Venice Biennale. An Experiment or Product of the Bourgeois Culture?", in *Relive Media Art Histories*, Cubitt, S., and Thomas, P. (Eds.) (Cambridge, Mass.: The MIT Press), pp. 119–134.

Franco, Francesca (2017). *Generative Systems Art: The Work of Ernest Edmonds* (Abingdon, Routledge).

Mohr, Manfred (1985). Artist's Statement, in Catalogue "Manfred Mohr Divisibility II Generative Arbeiten 1981–1984" (Cologne: Galerie Teufel, 1985), n.p.

Molnar, Vera (1995). "My Mother's Letters: Simulation by Computer", *Leonardo*, Vol. 28, No. 3, pp. 167–170.

Nake, Frieder (1971). "There Should Be No Computer Art", in *Computer Art Society's Bulletin PAGE*, No. 18, October 1971, n.p. Available online at http://www.bbk.ac.uk/hosted/cache/archive/PAGE/PAGE18.pdf. [Accessed 27 August 2018].

Verostko, Roman (2017). "San Marco Apocalypse: Lifting the Veil", Artist's statement produced on the occasion of the exhibition *Algorithmic Signs* (Venice, 2017). Available online at http://www.verostko.com/archive/shows-gr/venice/apoc-sm2017.pdf. [Accessed 27 August 2018].

Chapter 2
Interview with Ernest Edmonds

Interview Recorded in London, 14 April 2016, and Venice, 21 October 2017

Ernest Edmonds has pioneered the field of computational art and contributed to the broader field of contemporary art from the late 1960s to the present. His innovative work has focussed on the invention of new concepts, tools and forms in the context of colour field painting and systems art. Born in London in 1942, he began painting at an early age and continued to do so throughout his formal education in mathematics, philosophy and logic. Throughout his life, he has made artworks with reflected as well as transmitted light, both painting and writing code to make interactive generative works. His work not only acknowledges a historical connection, often overlooked, to the structural research undertaken by constructivist artists in the twentieth century, but also demonstrates that the points made by this past tradition could be extended into the digital age in a powerful and enduring investigation of mathematical and computational systems. By applying colour theory, computational logic and programmed systems to his work, Edmonds combined the structural research of Charles Biederman and the constructivists with Matisse's use of colour for the first time, and took them to a new level encompassing time, colour and interaction. The digital process gave generative art new possibilities and brought new opportunities for Edmonds, allowing him to create systems in which artworks have a life of their own.

He has exhibited computer-based and systems art around the world since 1970 and showed the first computer-generated video at Exhibiting Space in 1985. Recent exhibitions have included *New Acquisitions*, Victoria and Albert Museum; *Light Logic*, Site Gallery, Sheffield; retrospectives in Beijing and Shanghai (2015); and *Primary Codes*, Rio de Janeiro (2015), as well as exhibitions in Sydney, Berlin, Riga, Olomouc and London. Edmonds has been a significant figure internationally across the disciplines of art, computing and logic, both as a practitioner and as a researcher, for over forty years, and remains highly active. He has vigorously extended the concept of art as visual research by developing a new approach to art practice that integrates research as a formal activity. In 2017, he was the recipient of the ACM SIGGRAPH Distinguished Artist Award for Lifetime Achievement in Digital Art and

© Springer Nature Switzerland AG 2022
F. Franco, *The Algorithmic Dimension*, Springer Series on Cultural Computing,
https://doi.org/10.1007/978-3-319-61167-9_2

the ACM SIGCHI Lifetime Achievement Award in Computer–Human Interaction Practice. His archives are collected by the Victoria and Albert Museum, as part of the National Archive of Computer-Based Art and Design.

The first part of the interview, conducted in 2016, explores how systems art, Systems Theory, and his personal relationships with artists such as Malcolm Hughes, Kenneth Martin and Edward Ihnatowicz influenced Edmonds' art practice. This interview was originally published, in a shorter version, by *Interdisciplinary Science Reviews* (Edmonds and Franco 2017). The second part of the interview was recorded in Venice during the opening of *Algorithmic Signs*, in 2017.

Francesca Franco: How did your art and systems interests start to come together and how did that lead to an interest in cybernetics and Systems Theory?

Ernest Edmonds: In the 1960s, I was working in parallel and separately really in art as an artist and in logic as a logician. This was just a two-pronged part of life. Both things were intellectually demanding, intellectually interesting, but not connected to start with. As time moved on I happened to be working at what became Leicester Polytechnic, working on logic, and discovered that they had one computer. Out of intellectual curiosity, I taught myself how to program it, so this was the third interest closely related to logic and not at that time related to art. I was interested in the constructivist tradition and when I was an undergraduate student, about 1963–64, I used mathematics to try to understand better a painting by Mondrian. I looked for mathematical systems underlying the painting. So I had, even then, tried to apply mathematical systems at least to understanding art and wondered whether any of those systems were used by Mondrian. My results were inconclusive in the sense of whether they were used or not, but I could grasp more about his works by looking through a mathematical window. Then, for various almost accidental reasons, I became a lecturer in Computer Science. Having taught myself how to program, the department I was working in was in need of a lecturer in Computing. There was this famous story about my using the computer to finish "Nineteen" (Fig. 2.1). At that time I met Stroud Cornock, which was important in terms of friendship, discussions and practice. I was interested in psychology, I was interested in systems and I discovered Systems Theory and the applications of Systems Theory in biology and psychology.

There was the beginning of a coming together—from logic, through Systems Theory and towards psychology, which started to bring it towards the realms of art. One thing I did was look at the projects that I was setting Computer Science students as part of their final-year degree program. I had an idea to say, to some students, "Would you like, as a project, to try to construct computer software that would be helpful to artists"? A couple of students decided they would do this. It was just one of those things that happen; I started this discussion with students and set them on the road to talking with artists to try to find out what was useful.

Stroud had come from working with Roy Ascott, so there was an indirect influence from Roy coming in here. I was also extremely aware of what was going on in happenings and the interest in participation. So at the end of the 1960s there was this confluence of logic, computing and Systems Theory with art—from the more formalised views of art-making through to theories of participation and interaction.

Fig. 2.1 Ernest Edmonds, "Nineteen", 1968–69. ©Ernest Edmonds. Image courtesy of Jules Lister

"Nineteen", "Communications Game",[1] and "*Datapack"[2] (Figs. 2.2 and 2.3) are works that exemplify this. This was the coming together, and I was not just involved with Stroud but also with other people who were interested in these boundaries. I think it was in the air at that time. If you look internationally you can see many people

---

[1] "Communications Game" (1970) represents Edmonds's original network communication art system conceived in 1970. The work included stations for a maximum of six participants. The stations were arranged so that participants could not see one another, but could see one or two stimulus-providing units within the station. Each unit could be acted upon by the participant in response to a given stimulus. No instructions were given to participants on the manner in which the system of units operated. The idea behind "Communications Game" was to see art as a communication or interaction between people enabled by technology.

[2] "*Datapack" (1970) represents an early interactive computer-based art system. The work was an example of a matrix that consists of participants, a display, a computer installation and a designated area around the Vickers Building next to the Tate Gallery in London. "*Datapack" was a system that allowed participants to have a "pseudo-English conversation" with the computer. The results of this conversation were then processed by the machine connected to a drum plotter. This was able to identify a volume of space around the Vickers Building (now known as the Millbank Tower) and allocate it to the active participant. Part of the output of this process was a drawing, made by the plotter, using impulses collated from the participant's data. "*Datapack" represents an early investigation into the potentially changing relationship between artist and viewer or "participant", accelerated by the intervention of the computer.

Fig. 2.2 Edmonds operating
Datapack, 1970. ©Ernest
Edmonds. Image courtesy of
the artist

around this time doing these kinds of things. There was this interest in bringing these things together and seeing what might flourish.

FF: Can you say what was the most important lesson you learnt from Systems Theory, in terms of your work then and over the following decades?

EE: I think probably the most important lesson was that one could understand what might look like random behaviour in terms of interactions between different systems, or one system and the outside world, you might say. So the notion of indeterminate activity could replace the notion of random activity. What this implied was that there could be structures and boundaries around possible behaviours that could be formed. You could imagine making an artwork where you did not know what was going to happen, what it was going to look like, sound like, or whatever, but you knew that it would be within a certain envelope, as it were. You could design the envelope and then what happened actually would depend upon the interactions between the systems. This is really based on notions of open systems as against closed systems. That meant that one could work with it, one could handle it, one could design it, one could consider the aesthetics of it and it became possible to imagine using systems as a medium in which to make art. Not that I knew how to do it or what it would be like, but there was this realisation that probably is the answer to your question.

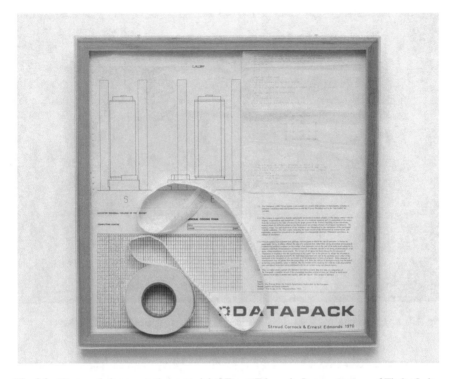

Fig. 2.3 *Datapack* documentation material. ©Ernest Edmonds. Image courtesy of Thales Leite

FF: If you could choose examples of your works from the 1960s and early 1970s that were inspired by this notion which would you choose?

EE: OK, the first was "*Datapack", which was a joint work made with Stroud Cornock. One of the things in "*Datapack", which resulted from anyone interacting with it, was a drawing made by a graph plotter from instructions in the computer (Fig. 2.3). We never knew what the drawing would be exactly, so it was as much a surprise to me, who wrote the code, as to Stroud, with whom I discussed the design; but nevertheless, we knew the aesthetic of the drawing, but the particularities of it were dependent entirely on the interactions that took place.

The second example would be one of the versions of "Communications Game". I knew that lights would flash and people would flick switches, but I did not know which light would flash at which time, because that depended on what people did. I just knew the processes and the constraints on those processes.

The third example is not electronic or computer art at all, it is a thing I made called "Jigsaw" around the same time (1970) (Fig. 2.4), which was a kind of jigsaw puzzle. I was seeing what could be done in this context without using the complexities of electronics or computers to make it as simple as possible. How could I deal with this complex notion in the simplest possible way? I came up with this idea of an artwork which consisted of pieces, apparently of a jigsaw, but that was different because it

Fig. 2.4 Ernest Edmonds, *Jigsaw*, 1970. ©Ernest Edmonds. Image courtesy of the artist

could be arranged with the pieces fitting together in very many different ways. There was not just one way of putting the pieces together, there were very many ways, so you could have this jigsaw on your table and you could change it. On different days it could look different, but it could still be fitted together. The fitting of it together provided constraints, so the aesthetics was determined but the particularities in which the pieces fitted were not, so that was an interesting example, I found.

FF: Not long after you joined Leicester Polytechnic, you were appointed as a Lecturer in Computer Science. What impact did that have on your art?

EE: Lots! I had already obtained access to the main Polytechnic's computer and taught myself to program it, as I said before, but any lecturer from any department could have done that if they wanted. But now, for example, I was part of the team that decided what the next computer to buy would be and what we might want to go with it. So I helped ensure that we had the kit that we used for "*Datapack". So my collaborations across the Polytechnic were enhanced. Then, of course, I was in a cultural climate where working with digital technology was normal, which certainly helped in my development and construction of the "Communications Game" series of works. Later on we built a display system that went beyond what could be bought at the time.

FF: Did teaching computing have any influence?

EE: Well, it forced me to learn more. One particular thing proved very important: the student project that I mentioned earlier. They applied the methods that they had been taught, starting by finding out what the requirements were before designing anything. However, this proved very problematic because the artists/designers kept changing their minds. The important thing was that I worked out that the software design method was wrong and that for art—mine very much included—we needed an iterative process.

FF: So did you invent one?

EE: Yes. To cut it short, I described it, without any problems, to the Computer Arts Society in 1969, but the computing world was harder to convince. I eventually published the idea, and it is sometimes seen as the start of what is now called "agile programming" or "agile design". In fact the approach is pretty normal in much of computing today. You could say that it is a more systems way of looking at software design.

FF: In your opinion, how important was the research into cybernetics for artistic practice?

EE: First of all, it was particularly interesting to discover a bunch of people around Brunel University who were very active in cybernetics and, related to this, people involved in the 1968 exhibition *Cybernetic Serendipity*[3]; Gordon Pask, for example. I do not think cybernetics had a direct influence beyond what I have been talking about on my art, except to say that it was showing that you could have a respectable science about this. In other words, it could be quite formal and we could deal with these matters in quite a formal and serious way. We could investigate and question the notions about how behaviours took place. Behind all this, the whole notion of behaviour coming within the realm of art, behaviour as an element to address as an artist was exciting. Cybernetics gave a clue as to how you might be able to do that, and that you might be able to do it.

FF: How did you get to know the work of the systems art group?

EE: Obviously I was familiar with a lot of work that was in the constructivist tradition and used systems of various kinds, but then there was a very important exhibition,

---

[3] *Cybernetic Serendipity* was an exhibition aiming at showing the main areas of experimentation and the creative use of technology in contemporary art. Curated by Jasia Reichardt at the Institute of Contemporary Art in London in 1968, it was introduced to the public as the "first international exhibition exploring and demonstrating some of the relationships between the arts and technology" (*ICA Bulletin*, August 1968). It included sections dedicated to computer-generated graphics, films, music and poetry; cybernetic devices and environments; remote control robots; and painting machines. Among the artists participating in the show were John H. Whitney, Michael Noll, the Computer Technique Group, Nicholas Schöffer, Frieder Nake, George Nees, Bridget Riley, Charles Csuri, K. C. Knowlton and Leon D. Harmon.

which was very revealing, the *Systems*[4] art exhibition which toured the UK. I saw it in London and Leicester and saw it more than once in each location: an interesting essay by Stephen Bann introduced the catalogue. This was important to me because it revealed that there was a group of artists in the UK working with systems to underpin their work. All these people were in fact producing static art objects and images, but they were using formal systems to generate those objects, to provide the structures behind them. Instead of just thinking about systems to produce behaviours, you could use systems to produce artworks. Of course we knew, for example, perspective and so on, but this was putting it in a modern context. And it turned out that I knew some of these people, so it was some coming together.

Two of the systems artists who were involved in that group, not necessarily in that particular exhibition, were working at Leicester Polytechnic and became friends of mine. I got to know other people in that group over the years. So this was a very important focal point for me in terms of the development of my art. It did not stop me being concerned with behaviours and interactive art and so on, but it broadened my interest and I looked back to how the formal methods that I had used in programming to construct "Nineteen" had application beyond just the way I used them then: not just to solve an aesthetic problem but to generate an aesthetic solution, which is a rather different way of looking at the process of making an artwork.

FF: Did you make anything at the time that was directly influenced by the *Systems* exhibition or your interaction with these friends and colleagues at Leicester?

EE: Some of the drawings I was doing in the early 1970s (Fig. 2.5), where I was constructing a geometric structure in which a particular line at a particular angle should occur in a particular place geometrically, and then adding to that a process structure about what order things should be done in. Then, making the drawing by hand, following the procedure that was defined and obeying the geometric structures that were underlying the work. In a way, what I was doing there was going a step further than what the systems artists were doing because, as well as using the system to define the geometric structure of the work, I was using systems also to define the procedure to be used to make the work. This became an important element for me, which came really from my knowledge of computer programming, and understanding of what computer programming can do. So I now had these two elements, the geometric structure and the process of making, both embedded in a "systems" view of making.

FF: How did you decide the angles of the lines that cross each other in these drawings? Can you tell me more about that?

---

[4] *Systeemi-System* was an exhibition originally organised by Jeffrey Steele in 1969 for the Amos Anderson Museum, Helsinki. From 1972 to 1973, *Systems*, a larger Arts Council exhibition, including more artists, toured the UK starting from the Whitechapel Art Gallery in London, and moving then to Manchester, Sheffield, Billingham, Newcastle, Birmingham, Leicester, Leeds, Southampton, Newport and Oxford. Artists included Richard Allen, John Ernest, Malcom Hughes, Colin Jones, Michael Kidner, Peter Lowe, James Moyes, David Saunders, Geoffrey Smedley, Jean Spencer, Jeffrey Steele and Gillian Wise Ciobotaru.

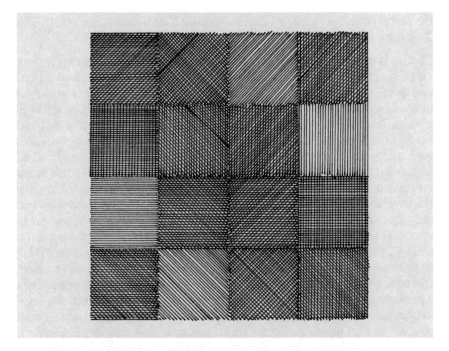

Fig. 2.5   Ernest Edmonds, *Untitled*, 1975. Museum no. E.864-2010. ©Victoria and Albert Museum, London/Ernest Edmonds. Image courtesy of the Victoria and Albert Museum, London

EE: There were many different instructions, so I will just give you one example. It was not always done this way but I will describe one way that I did it. So maybe I have a matrix of 3 by 3 squares and I would say that the top left will have horizontal lines and that all of the squares that were on the same column or row would also have horizontal lines and so on; then maybe the bottom square in the middle would have 45-degree lines upwards and every square in that row or column should also have lines at that angle and then that would mean that the middle square in the third column would have some other line angled in another direction and that line angled would be copied in all of the row and column that was involved. So now we have a geometrical structure that is rigorously defined. If the process leads to my drawing in more than one direction in a particular square, then you get overlapping.

FF: So, aesthetically, what were you looking for?

EE: A tension, really. I learnt primarily from Mondrian about asymmetry and how you can get balance with tension through using asymmetry and this was taking that notion in principle, not in detail, in another way forward. There is no real symmetry, in fact it is rigorously defined to avoid any kind of symmetry. But it is tight, and the visual tension is almost something disturbing to look at: challenging, intriguing.

FF: This reminds me of the process that Kenneth Martin used to create his works. Do you see any analogy?

EE: This is very interesting because these notions were very embedded in my work. It is difficult for me to recall now when I first saw Kenneth's work, but it would have been almost certainly in the late 1960s. In the early days when I saw his work I was intrigued by it and loved it from the outset, but I don't know that I understood it in the depth that I came to much later, especially after I met him and talked to him. So I think that the mechanics behind the magic of the art was something that I only understood later, but the fact that it was magical was obvious to me from the outset. What I think ended up appealing to me a great deal was the clarity of thinking that he had that led to the making of his work, which was something that very much was at one with the kind of things that I was trying to do using either computer programming or computational notions, mathematical procedural ways of making works using clear processes to generate the work without ornament and side parts. There was a sort of classical clarity in his work. I had added this idea of process to the systems used by the systems artists, but Kenneth was in fact also using rigorous processes in making his works. Now, actually, he used randomness—picking numbers out of a hat kind of randomness—which I did not do, but that was a minor point. The most important point was that he was defining a systematic process of making; not just how it should look, not just the geometry, but the making process. This was very important in my drawings and in those sprayed paintings and, of course, also in the computer-based works which were time-based and interactive. In the computer-based works of mine (time-based and interactive ones), images are being made all the time, so the processes of making are integral to the work. I think this approach to make was really important, and his work was extremely influential for me.

FF: So I guess you felt quite relieved to see his work.

EE: Absolutely, because I felt less alone and there was someone I could learn from: the systems art people in the first place, and then Kenneth in particular. He was not part of the systems art group, but he made me feel much more connected and grounded in the work I was doing, and I have always felt that a historical grounding is really important for an artist.

FF: Are there any works that you recall having done under the specific influence of Kenneth?

EE: What Kenneth made me realise was that I should not give up painting, because when I first met him it was just at that time that I discovered I could do time-based work using systems. The reason for this, naturally, was to do with the development of the technology. His influence was to keep in my mind that, using the same concepts and ideas, and dealing with the same aesthetics, I could continue to make paintings, make marks on canvas and produce images to deal with many of the same issues. That stayed with me, so I still do.

FF: Can you tell us about a work that still reflects those ideas?

Fig. 2.6 Ernest Edmonds, *Four from Shaping Space*, 2012. ©Ernest Edmonds. Image courtesy of GV Art, London

EE: If you look at any of my recent four-part paintings they all relate, not in an obvious visual way but conceptually, to Kenneth and what he taught me (Fig. 2.6). The point is that if you look at one of those works you cannot work out why this colour square is there. It actually does not matter, it is there for very specific systems reasons, and Kenneth had very good reasons for why a particular colour was in a particular place in his paintings.

FF: How did your work evolve after that?

EE: There were two important changes in the next decade or two. First of all, right at the beginning of the 1980s, the realisation that I could make time-based work. I was very familiar with systems artists making series of works. You could almost think of these as a series of stills in a film. I started to work on using my systems to make time-based work, to take the process of making and turning that into the process of evolution, during time, of a work. So that process became part of the work instead of just part of the making. On the side, this could incorporate the interaction, that I had been interested in earlier, in a nice way.

The second thing, that happened a bit later, was the realisation that I could formalise my dealing with colour. I could start to apply these systems approaches to the selection, generation and change of colour in a work as well as to all the other aspects.

FF: Would you like to talk about the lesson you learnt from Malcolm Hughes?

EE: I liked Malcolm Hughes' work very much. He was one of the artists in the Systems group who I admired but he was also very important as an educator and as an influence on others, because he had a strong theoretical base and a strong vision of the future. He and I had many discussions, which I value greatly, in which he helped me work out more precisely what I was trying to do, to make explicit what was on my mind. He helped to put the developments of work using computer programming, for example, in the context of systems art in particular and the general development of twentieth-century abstract art. Malcolm was very aware, from a long time ago, of the importance of the computer as something with potential, which is why he bought one for the course that he ran at the Slade. This led to the Slade postgraduate diploma being a very important hotbed for the development of computer-based art based upon Malcolm's vision. He got the right students, he hired the right people; this was very much his way. He knew quite a lot about what we were doing in Leicester at the time, and he definitely saw what we were doing as important for the future. He cemented my confidence in the developments we were engaged in as a group and my personal confidence that what I was doing was rooted and properly grounded in twentieth-century art.

FF: Can you tell me more about your connection with Edward Ihnatowicz?

EE: I first met Edward in 1971 at the *Invention of Problems II* exhibition and Symposium that Stroud Cornock organised at Leicester Polytechnic. That was an interesting time. I also met Steve Willats, John Lifton and many other interesting artists. Edward and I got to know one another quite well and met and had very engaged conversations about interaction and the nature of interaction as a subject of art, as a medium itself. We talked about the way that an interactive artwork could be constructed and we also talked about things that are sometimes seen as artificial intelligence subjects or cognitive science subjects, which turned out to be important to art. For example, the relationship between touching and perceiving, the way in which by acting we affect what we perceive. This was very interesting because it is something that I still have not incorporated deeply into my art, and Edward never did, but he might well have done by now had he been still alive. He was definitely very concerned with this direction. His work showed how very simple mechanisms that drove the behaviour of an artwork could lead to very persuasive, engaging and challenging behaviours. This is something that relates to some work by cognitive scientists, for example, that sometimes can show how it is possible to postulate that relatively simple rule-based mechanisms can lead to behaviours that are seen as very natural.

I remember being with him at a conference and exhibition that were organised by the Computer Arts Society in Edinburgh in 1973.[5] At the conference I was presenting my work "Communications Game" and Edward was showing "The Bandit". And all the time we were talking about interaction and the nature of interaction and the nature of artificial intelligence and what it meant to respond to human behaviour in some ways that would seem meaningful to human beings. "The Bandit" might be said to be something moving a bit in the direction of a concern for action and perception because, as you moved it, it made a note of the movements that you made and then moved itself back, repeating those motions, so you have this kind of dialogue between your actions and its actions. Or, if you like, from "The Bandit"'s point of view, there was a dialogue between what it was doing and what the human was doing physically. The "intelligent" behaviour of "The Bandit" was very much intimately connected to movement, contact and action. This is less obviously so in "SAM", but Edward's thinking was very much in this direction and had he lived longer he would have made works, I think, that explored these matters.

FF: In terms of your work, how did these matters and ideas influence you at that time?

EE: I think they influenced my ideas for "Communications Game", which I developed through the early 1970s, starting around 1970. But I was still working on these ideas at the time of the Edinburgh conference and beyond. Where the human action was integrated with the behaviour of the whole art system, the human behaviour was integral to the very nature of the artwork. But, like Edward, I was influenced by a broader understanding of the field and my thinking about what might come in the future, and this did not just materialise in a fully fledged form within the works for some time.

FF: How did your work evolve as a result of these concerns? Is there an example you could single out?

EE: Those discussions with Edward were to consolidate my interest in interactive art in the sense of taking full account of modelling or using metaphors of living behaviours, so that I was not driven by the technology and by artificial intelligence. I was driven, and still am, much more by my observations and understanding of human and animal behaviour.

FF: In April 1976, you organised an AISB meeting called Human & Robot Behaviour at Leicester Polytechnic (Collett 1977). Among the invited talks was one by Edward Ihnatowicz in which he put forward his argument about the integral significance of the body in intelligent behaviour. As you noted, it was quite far-reaching in intent, "… we are interested not so much in machines that can learn but in machines that can teach, or at least in machines that can teach, having learnt". This presentation

---

in Leicester was possibly Edward's most public statement at that time, where he anticipated many future developments in the interactive arts. Where did the idea of that meeting come from?

EE: As always in my life, I have been working with more than one community. At that time I was working with the CAS people, the Royal College of Art, the Slade and so on. I was working in an art community interested in the exploitation of technology or the implications of technology for art. At the same time I was a member of AISB, which was essentially, and still is, a society interested in artificial intelligence in general and with robotics as one of its subjects of interest. The main group at that time was at Edinburgh University, but people in other places, like in Sussex, for example, were also making important contributions. I made a proposal to AISB that we hold a meeting in Leicester to bring these communities together. We started the Creativity and Cognition series of conferences in 1993 for a similar kind of motivation. Human & Robot Behaviour was an early example of me bringing different communities together. People came from the Royal College of Art, from Edinburgh University, etc. It was a meeting place for people from a robotic and cognitive science background with people from an art and technology background. I invited Edward to be one of the speakers, and he gave a talk about his theoretical position. This was an attempt to spark off creative thought, bringing these communities together. In some ways, maybe regrettably, for a long time Edward was better known in the robotics community than in the art world, although his real contribution was to art. I think he was a very important early maker of interactive art, with a very serious intent for dealing with matters of life, living behaviours, human and animal life.

FF: Is there a work of yours that encapsulates all these influences, systems art, Systems Theory, cybernetics?

EE: It is difficult to answer this question because the only way to answer is through the work that I have not finished, that I am working on now. Maybe that is always going to be the answer to such a question by any artist. This work, which is currently labelled "Open Spaces", is the one that I think best achieves that. It is a multipart work where the parts consist of cameras, screens, projected images separated at least around a building, but perhaps around a city or the world, as a single work. All those parts communicate with one another wirelessly and interact with one another. So, for example, the movement in one space influences what is seen in another. The point is that this starts to combine the systemisation of colour and so on with the communications game idea. All of the concepts that I have been working with are beginning to come together in a single work. This feels like an important step that encapsulates those influences and interests.

FF: How important are rules and logic in your work, and how does your audience perceive them?

EE: This is a very important question, but let me try to give you a quick answer. The rules are crucial. The art is actually made from that, and there are people who are interested in ways of making those rules very obvious. The most worn-out current activity is in music with live coding, where people show the program on the screen while they are actually changing the program so you are listening to music, seeing the program and so on. Mostly people can't understand by looking at that code what the structure really is anyway, but that's a way that people are addressing the problem today. I think in the end it is what the work resolves in that counts. I believe you can love Bach without understanding fugues, you can love Webern without understanding all the arithmetic of serial music. This doesn't mean to say you might not gain benefits from knowing more, but neither Bach nor Webern, to take these two as an example, show you the rules in the sound. It is not exactly an unusual position to say, "Well, I'm afraid you can't see what the rules are here", but the psychological theories around this suggest that in good works you do have a sense that you understand the structure. That tension in the work, almost knowing, or seeing, that it is not random and that there is some structure there, having some idea of it, but not being able to deduce it directly from the work itself, maybe actually contributes significantly to the experience. It's a big question, it's an open question and people are exploring it in all sorts of different ways as we speak.

FF[6]: We are very honoured to have your works exhibited here in Venice. How do you feel about showing your work in this environment?

EE: It's great to show my work here. First, because it is in this beautiful city with great traditions, but also because it is in a great context, with my friends who all started to use computers and algorithms in their art at roughly the same period, and I think that all of our works are much enriched by being seen in this context, and I find that it is better to understand our work in context than in isolation.

FF: In your room, we have a selection of works from several phases of your career as an artist. I'd like to know what your first feeling was when you realised you could use the computer to make art?

EE: Well, the first time I did it was to solve a problem, so in a way it was a simple thing to do. This was in 1968. But as soon as I did that, I realised that it was a much richer seam to delve into than I had ever thought before. There were two things that emerged over the following two years. One was the more rigorous dealing with systems and algorithms in art. Cézanne talked about systems and so did Malevich, and there was of course the Systems group in England. So the idea of using algorithms in some sense was there, but I was very interested in the rigorous use of algorithms. I was interested in the philosophy of mathematics and the importance of the algorithm and the invention of computation as a new concept in human thinking. So it seemed to me that it provided an opportunity for a new conceptualisation of ourselves and aesthetics. So that was the main thing that it offered, which became a lifelong pursuit for me, and not only me of course. The second thing was that when you embedded computation into the computer, then it had other special properties. A computer can act as a control device and it can manipulate things that interact with the world. New

---

[6] Venice interview from this point onwards.

possibilities emerged about interactive art, and later distributed art. So that was a second theme that began for me at that time.

FF: So what were your feelings when you realised that?

EE: I felt excited, I felt experimental. I was already painting in an experimental way, but suddenly, that became much stronger, and the earlier experiments seemed very mild and uninteresting in comparison. It so happened that I was able to have access to technology and algorithmic stuff, and I had some capability in that area, so that I could really explore it by developing new forms of computation, new algorithmic methods and new computer technologies in order to feed this mission that I have developed to pursuit my artistic developments.

FF: And, in terms of the technology available at that time, did you ever feel the need of something that was not available yet, or did you use what was already in place?

EE: I needed things that were not available. I started by using a computer that could not have possibly fitted in this room. It was much too big, and it was a computer that was technologically much smaller than a watch is today. And dealing with interaction was really difficult, there were no PCs … However, I was very involved in the community of computer development and very involved in doing that work, so I could see that we had a future. By 1970 I had set myself a program of work that would only be realisable sensibly in the early 1980s. I could see that was coming, and I have always been more interested in the conceptual than the technological side—I'm not a techie hacker sort of person, I am much more of a philosophical–conceptual person, so my art is based more on that side of life. I used a phrase very often, "technology intersection", that means just doing all the work you have to do, even though it might take some years before the technology that one needs is actually available.

FF: What about now, again in terms of the technology available? How do you feel about that?

EE: The technology available today is amazing. It has a downside in a sense that it is easy to produce stuff that is pretty and that is deeply uninteresting, but for me it has expanded all that is possible, so I have been able to go into new areas that I think are really important: not just exploring interaction and time, but now connectivity and distribution. You can have an artwork that extends over the whole world and interacts with the whole world. This is a future that is really important.

FF: I would also like to ask you a question about your work "Growth and Form" (Figs. 2.7, 2.8, 2.9 and 2.10) that we commissioned especially for this exhibition. Can you describe all the processes involved in this work?

EE: First of all, I should say that a great concern of mine as an artist, and as for many other artists, is colour. And an innovation that I made, that has been really important to me, is to systematise my dealing with colour. I don't anymore deal with colour by tweaking it, I use the kind of mathematical system that people use to create

Fig. 2.7 Ernest Edmonds, four still images from *Growth and Form* as installed at "Algorithmic Signs", Venice 2017. ©Ernest Edmonds. Image courtesy of Pier Parimbelli

Fig. 2.8 Ernest Edmonds, four still images from *Growth and Form* as installed at "Algorithmic Signs", Venice 2017. ©Ernest Edmonds. Image courtesy of Pier Parimbelli

shapes to create colour and sets of colours. This is a massively invaluable thing for me. One thing is dealing with colour using set of rules—so it is generative art. At the core of the artwork is a set of rules that determine what you see on the screen at any one moment, and the computer follows those rules; and some of those rules deal with selecting the colour—should the hues shift a little bit?, should the intensity

Fig. 2.9 Ernest Edmonds, four still images from *Growth and Form* as installed at "Algorithmic Signs", Venice 2017. ©Ernest Edmonds. Image courtesy of Pier Parimbelli

Fig. 2.10 Ernest Edmonds, four still images from *Growth and Form* as installed at "Algorithmic Signs", Venice 2017. ©Ernest Edmonds. Image courtesy of Pier Parimbelli

of the colour increase or decrease?—and so on. For "Growth and Form", because of its location, the colours are, for me, relatively distant in respect of the hues and relatively bright. That is because it is an installation piece, and of course you have to take the context into account. The colour looks rather different from other works in my room. The timings—like "does it go fast or slow?"—are also systematised, as is often done in music, so it is musical, you might say. The third thing is, the widths of the stripes, the selection of stripes, is also systematised. So, first, the whole thing is generative, driven by a set of rules. The second thing is that there is a camera up there watching, watching for movement. The most obvious thing is that, when the computer detects people coming in or going out, it interferes with the generative process, so that there are some reactions. Not a simple reaction where someone can see their face, but the colours change suddenly. So there is a response that people who are sensitive enough would definitely spot. And there is a second level, which is more subtle and much more difficult to see, but is more interesting to me, which is that the rules are slowly changed so that the experience that the work has over the period of the exhibition will lead aspects of the colours or their shapes to change somewhat. The work will be a slightly different work at the end of the exhibition from what it was at the beginning.

FF: So is there a relationship between the colours you chose for this work and the site in which it is installed?

EE: This was a very difficult aspect of the work. I made a number of experiments in my studio. I had photographs of the site, and my first thought was to use the colours that I found in this space, and I experimented with that. And here is where the normal artistic intuition comes in, because my judgement looking at those colours was that really did not create a very interesting work and that it was best to turn it on its head and choose something really quite different. In fact, if you look carefully, some of the hues in there can be found in that space, but the intensities and the brightness associated with those hues are quite different. And then, something I also do, is, as well as having some colours that are relatively close together, I'll have "wild card" colours that are very different, and so that's nice too. So "Growth and Form" relates to the colours in the space, without copying them, just as it relates to the movements without imitating them. In this way, I hope that it integrates with but extends the space.

This interview has helped in clarifying a number of key steps in Edmonds' artistic career. One factor that contributed in seeing the computer not just as a mere "assistant" or a tool that facilitates complex calculations to solve mathematical problems, was when Edmonds realised that the computer was a tool that would enable him to connect his two main passions, art and logic, previously seen as two complete separate entities. Using the computer as a tool to analyse a painting by Mondrian, allowed Edmonds not only to visualise mathematical systems underlying the painting. This encouraged him to look at art through a mathematical perspective and to bring logic and Systems Theory towards the realm of art.

One more factor that had a strong impact on how Edmonds' art developed is the input that a network of friends, colleagues, artists and mentors coming from different disciplines and backgrounds had on Edmonds' creativity. Just to name some key lessons learnt from this particular aspect that developed into long-term creative outputs, one is the notion of participation and interaction, thanks to Cornock and

Ascott. Another important lesson learnt was how different systems interact, thanks to Systems Theory and the discovery of a group of artists, the systems art group, that made Edmonds realise he was not alone in seeing art as the result of formal generative systems, and that he could use systems to produce artworks. Finding a common language between different disciplines and working with more than one community have helped Edmonds in exploiting technology for art and to expand his creativity for over fifty years, up to the present time.

The following photos are of artwork on display at the exhibition, the figure number refers to the number on the map of the floor plan of exhibition which can be viewed in Chap. 7.

4. Ernest Edmonds, *Growth and Form*, 2017, Computer-based interactive installation

52. Ernest Edmonds, *Fifty-Seven*, 1982–1984, acrylic on canvas, 122 × 122 cm

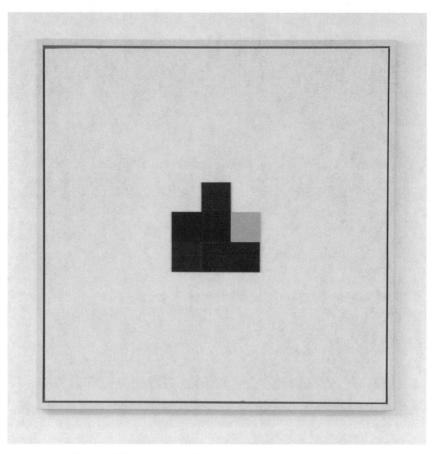

53. Ernest Edmonds, *Forty-Five*, 1975, cellulose relief, 60 × 60 cm

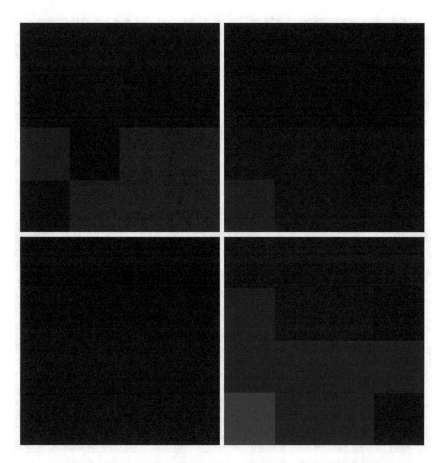

54. Ernest Edmonds, *Four Shaping Forms*, 2017, aluminium, 120 × 120 cm

55. Ernest Edmonds, *Fifty-Two*, 1980, acrylic on canvas 92 × 92 cm each

56. Ernest Edmonds, *Twenty-One*, 1976–1977, ink on paper, 56 × 56 cm

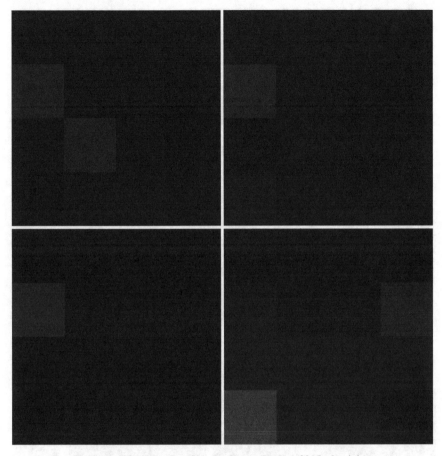

57. Ernest Edmonds, *Four Shaping Forms (Venice)*, 2015, aluminium

58. Ernest Edmonds, *Nagoya*, 1996, generative video

59. Ernest Edmonds, *Shaping Form*, 2015, generative interactive video

60. Ernest Edmonds, *Shaping Form*, 2015, generative interactive video

61. Ernest Edmonds, *Shaping Form*, 2007, generative interactive video, screen

62. Ernest Edmonds, *Shaping Space*, 2012, interactive installation

References

Collett, Arnold J. (1977). "Report on the 1976 Conference on Human and Robot Behaviour at Leicester Polytechnic, England", *Leonardo*, Vol. 10, No. 1, p. 33. Available online at https://muse.jhu.edu/article/598476. [Accessed 26 August 2018].

Edmonds, Ernest, and Franco, Francesca (2017). "Systems Theory, Systems Art and the Computer: Ernest Edmonds Interviewed by Francesca Franco", *Interdisciplinary Science Reviews*, Vol. 42, Nos. 1–2, pp. 169–179.

Further Reading

Franco, Francesca, "Exploring Creative Intersections: Ernest Edmonds and his time-based generative art," *Digital Creativity*, Vol. 24, No. 3, 222–236 (2013).

Franco, Francesca, *Generative Systems Art: The Work of Ernest Edmonds*, Routledge, 2018.

Chapter 3
Interview with Manfred Mohr

Interview Recorded in New York, 29 October 2016, and Venice, 21 October 2017

Manfred Mohr is a pioneer of computer-generated algorithmic art. After discovering Max Bense's "Information Aesthetics" in the early 1960s, Mohr's artistic thinking radically changed. Within a few years, his art transformed from abstract expressionism to computer-generated algorithmic geometry. Encouraged by the computer-music composer Pierre Barbaud, whom he met in 1967, Mohr programmed his first computer drawings in 1969.

Some of the collections in which he is represented include the Centre Pompidou, Paris; Joseph Albers Museum, Bottrop; Mary and Leigh Block Museum of Art, Chicago; Victoria and Albert Museum, London; Ludwig Museum, Cologne; Wilhelm-Hack-Museum, Ludwigshafen; Kunstmuseum Stuttgart, Stuttgart; Stedelijk Museum, Amsterdam; Museum im Kulturspeicher, Würzburg; Kunsthalle Bremen, Bremen; Musée d'Art Moderne et Contemporain, Strasbourg; Daimler Contemporary, Berlin; Musée d'Art Contemporain, Montréal; Borusan Art Collection, Istanbul; McCrory Collection, New York; Esther Grether Collection, Basel; and Thoma Art Foundation, Chicago.

Mohr's work has been featured in many one-person shows and retrospectives in museums and galleries, such as ARC—Musée d'Art Moderne de la Ville de Paris, Paris 1971; Joseph Albers Museum, Bottrop 1998; Wilhelm-Hack-Museum, Ludwigshafen 1987 and 2002; Museum for Concrete Art, Ingolstadt 2001; Kunsthalle Bremen, Bremen 2007; Museum im Kulturspeicher, Würzburg 2005; Grażyna Kulczyk Fundacja, Poznań 2007; ZKM—Media Museum, Karlsruhe 2013; Featured Artist at Art Basel, Basel 2013; Center for the Arts, Virginia Tech 2014; Simons Center Gallery, Stony Brook 2015; Kunstverein, Pforzheim 1988 and 2008; and Museum Pforzheim Gallery, Pforzheim 1998 and 2017.

He took part in many group shows, including, among others, those at MoMA—Museum of Modern Art, New York 1980; Centre Pompidou, Paris 1978 and 1992; ZKM, Karlsruhe 2005, 2008 and 2010; Whitechapel Gallery, London 2016; CCCB, Barcelona 2016; Kunstmuseum Stuttgart, Stuttgart 2005, 2009, 2011, 2012, 2015, 2016 and 2017; Museum Ritter, Waldenbuch 2005, 2006, 2008 and 2013; Centro Cultural de la Villa, Madrid 1989; MoCA, Los Angeles 1975; National Museum of

© Springer Nature Switzerland AG 2022
F. Franco, *The Algorithmic Dimension*, Springer Series on Cultural Computing,
https://doi.org/10.1007/978-3-319-61167-9_3

Modern Art, Tokyo 1984; Museum of Modern Art, San Francisco 1973, 1977 and 1980; MoMA-PS1, New York 2008; MACM—Musée d'Art Contemporain, Montréal 1974, 1985 and 2013; Fundación Banco Santander, Madrid 2014; Muzeum Sztuki, Łódź 1981 and 2011; Neue Nationalgalerie, Berlin 1999; New Tendencies 5 at the Contemporary Art Gallery, Zagreb 1973; Leo Castelli Gallery, New York 1978; and Galerie Paul Facchetti, Paris 1965 and Zürich 1970.

Among the awards he received are the ACM SIGGRAPH Distinguished Artist Award for Lifetime Achievement in Digital Art, 2013; [ddaa] d.velop Digital Art Award, Berlin 2006; Artist Fellowship, New York Foundation of the Arts, New York 1997; Golden Nica from Ars Electronica, Linz 1990; and Camille Graeser-Preis, Zürich 1990.

Francesca Franco: From the timeline in your biography there are some dates that were crucial in the development of your art. I'd like to go through some of them with you. To start with, 1961 is an important date because that's around the time when you were first introduced to Max Bense's *Information Aesthetics*. How did this influence your thinking and creativity?

Manfred Mohr: It changed my life. I started out as an abstract expressionist, and, coming also from a music background, I knew that I could write down an idea on a music sheet. But in abstract expressionism, the result of one's work is usually accidental. Sometimes you have to make ten drawings before you make a good one, and that bothered me profoundly—that everything was based on an accident. I was looking for something that would put me in control of that aspect, but I didn't know which direction to take. Then I came upon Max Bense's philosophy. He essentially said that in our time we should create a "rational art", and that hit me profoundly. I started to ask myself, "What is rational"? I continued working on my abstract art but started slowly putting geometric forms into it, like a little square or straight lines or triangles, and every time I did that I thought, "Okay, this is rational". But of course it wasn't as simple as that. My art was getting more systematic, more geometric, but it was not rational, or, rather, its content was not rational. By 1965–66, when I completely constructed my work using geometrical forms made with a ruler and compass, the works were rationally constructed but their content was still not rational.

It was only in 1967, when I met Pierre Barbaud, a pioneer of computer music, that I finally understood that I had to write algorithms and programs, a logical procedure which runs on a computer to create a rational construct, and that entity was exactly what I was looking for. I started learning programming, and within one year I was ready to write my first program. I still had no computer and was desperately looking for one. It was not easy at the time because nobody had a computer or a plotter; they were large and expensive, and only big institutions could afford them. In 1969, when I was writing my first algorithms and making drawings and sculptures as part of the group "art et informatique" at the University of Paris in Vincennes, we had only a small computer and no plotter. One day I saw on French television that the Institute of Meteorology in Paris had just gotten a large electronic drawing table to draw their weather maps. That was exactly what I was looking for. I went there and asked if I could use their equipment. They didn't exactly receive me with open arms, but they

Fig. 3.1 Manfred Mohr at
the Institute of Meteorology
in Paris, 1970. ©Manfred
Mohr. Images courtesy of the
artist

told me to write a letter to the Ministry of Transportation, which I did. A few weeks later I received an answer, and I had an interview with the minister; he was very nice to me (I later discovered his childhood dream was to become an artist), and, since nobody had ever approached them with the crazy idea of using a computer and a plotter to make art, they granted me access to their laboratory. I worked there for thirteen years almost every night (Figs. 3.1, 3.2, 3.3 and 3.4).

That was the first step. Now I had the machines, but I still had to figure out what I really wanted to do. I decided to go back to my music background and found inspiration there for my initial ideas of programming my art. I did exactly what I did when I was writing music scores. I started writing linear developments, and I saw that I was very good at it. I made hundreds of drawings; some are exhibited in *Algorithmic Signs* here in Venice. Programming these works was like writing with an alphabet from left to right, this time not as a music score but as visual music where the direction of the drawing could go forward to an extent but could also go backward. It was not a music score to play but one to see.

FF: How did you feel about your first drawings made using a computer?

MM: When I made my first drawings with a pen plotter, I felt proud that I had done something I had not drawn myself. The machine had done it from my program. I remember showing my results to my friends and galleries, saying, "Look, I didn't do it, a machine did it". But they couldn't understand the satisfaction I got out of the fact that I could write down a logic and then that logic became visual, since the idea of my work is based on inventing an algorithm.

Fig. 3.2 Manfred Mohr at
the Institute of Meteorology
in Paris, 1970. ©Manfred
Mohr. Images courtesy of the
artist

Fig. 3.3 Manfred Mohr at
the Institute of Meteorology
in Paris, 1970. ©Manfred
Mohr. Images courtesy of the
artist

I know what the algorithm should do, but I don't know what the result will look like. After writing a program and running it on a computer, I'm always surprised by what I get out of the machine. When I wrote my first program in 1969, I didn't have a plotter yet, so a friend of mine in New York who had access to a light pen plotter at Brookhaven National Laboratory offered to run my program there. He sent me

Fig. 3.4 Manfred Mohr at
the Institute of Meteorology
in Paris, 1970. ©Manfred
Mohr. Images courtesy of the
artist

back a large selection of small plotter drawings on photo paper from my algorithm. I
remember I laid them down on the floor and looked at them, completely stunned by
this overwhelming output. I couldn't believe I could get all these possibilities from
a single algorithm. For me that was a revelation: the logic is what counts.

FF: That was a big step in your career. What was the most important lesson you
learned from it?

MM: I understood that, whatever I wanted to do, I first had to write the program to do
it. So if I wanted to draw a circle I had to go to a math book and look up a function for
a circle and write a program that draws a circle. It was a big change in my thinking.
It's not my hand that makes the drawing, it's my brain. Before I used a computer
and plotter, I was drawing freehand, but then I got more and more geometric and I
started using rulers and compass and masking tape to paint straight lines. It was a
very slow approach because I had to learn for myself what I thought "rational" could
be. I knew that was the direction I wanted to go but didn't yet know how to proceed.

FF: How did you know that was the direction?

MM: Because I started to understand that writing a program, i.e. inventing a logic,
would represent my artistic ideas. To write an algorithm is to invent rules. Anything
can be an algorithm, like getting up in the morning, putting on your shoes, brushing
your teeth, etc. An algorithm is a set of rules that has a beginning and an end. Once
I really understood that, my whole thinking changed. At first I went back to my
early paintings and other drawings I had done and started analysing those elements
like horizontal, vertical, or 45-degree lines, zigzag or square-wave repetitions and

Fig. 3.5 Manfred Mohr, *P-122*, 1972. ©Manfred Mohr. Image courtesy of the artist

differences in angles. All became significant in my set of rules. For example, I programmed a set of short lines distributed horizontally from left to right that could vary in angles, where each angle was attributed to a letter from the alphabet. I thus could write a visual text.

FF: Is there a work that encapsulates these ideas that you find particularly important from that phase of your career?

MM: Yes, for example "P-122" from 1972 (Fig. 3.5).

FF: When you switched to that approach, did you see abstract expressionism as a dead end?

MM: Not as a dead end, but definitely not my future. I still like abstract expressionism. I understand it well, but I want more control of what I am doing. I went away from expressionism even though I am still emotionally attached to it and somehow feel it hides in my work.

FF: In 1967, you met Pierre Barbaud, who encouraged you to program your first computer drawings, in 1969. What was the most important lesson you learned from him?

MM: That I had great control over what I did. The absolute novelty for me was that I do not have a visual image in mind, but a process which becomes visual. When I write an instruction, I have only a vague idea how it will look. Only after I run a program on a computer can I see the full results. That's a revolution in art—that one starts not visually but logically to do something. There was a big change in my mindset. I started to look at other people's work, searching for a logic, getting upset when I realised that there was no logic, just emotions. Until today, when I look at something, the first thing I look for is how the work is constructed, what is the logic behind it. So my world has changed completely, and I can't go back. Because I understood that knowledge is irreversible: once you know something you cannot not know it. I became a different person.

FF: When you decided that this was the route to take, what was the first message or content that you wanted to deliver through the computer in your art?

MM: It was, in the first place, a learning process for me also. I wasn't accomplished immediately, and today I'm still looking and learning new things. The confidence to write computer programs that would render my artistic ideas—that was my biggest step.

FF: Was it like learning a new language?

MM: Yes, exactly. Like learning a language. And if you can speak that language, you can express different things, so my idea was also that, if I could speak this language (learn to program), I could express exactly what I wanted to do. If I need an engineer, I have to explain to him what I want, then he comes with his psychology and changes things around. My original idea might get altered. At the beginning it was very rare that artists learned to program. So the fact that I learned and thus I knew what I was doing was a very good thing. I was very proud of this.

FF: 1969 was probably one of your busiest years, with the publication of your visual book *Artificiata I*, with your last hand drawing and the first drawings made with the aid of the computer.

MM: ARTIFICIATA I was a visual suite without any systematic logic; it was a development of visual signs from light to dark. After I finished it, I thought of doing an ARTIFICIATA II with a computer, this time with an internal logic. It took me forty years to get into the same mindset of doing an ARTIFICIATA II. About four years ago, I was working on an unrelated visual problem that dealt with a development in time. This was exactly what I wanted to do with ARTIFICIATA II, and so I decided I was ready for it (Fig. 3.6).

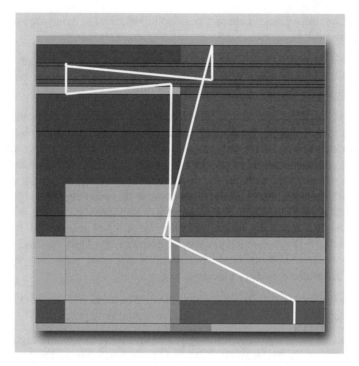

Fig. 3.6 Manfred Mohr, *P-1611_65-60,* 2012. ©Manfred Mohr. Image courtesy of the artist

FF: What was the alphabet, or the syntax, you chose in this new language?

MM: The alphabet was the hypercube and its possibilities, like calculating diagonal paths through this complex structure and like showing all the possible projections in 2D. That became my alphabet.

Going back in time: how I developed my alphabets, from my earliest programs, which were linear writings, to the present, I went through many stages. In my linear drawings of the early 1970s, each drawing represented a different idea and was not connected to the other drawings. My aim was to find a uniting idea to connect these drawings. Whenever I have to solve a problem, music comes to my mind. For example, when I play a saxophone, whatever music I play sounds like a saxophone. So I asked myself, "Why could I not invent an instrument that does graphics instead of sounds"? I had the idea of going back to the most basic form, the Cartesian coordinates, which is the cube. The cube became my instrument, and I started "playing" with it as I would do with a musical instrument. So my initial alphabet was the twelve lines of the cube. Then slowly over the years I expanded this first alphabet into a four-dimensional hypercube, which is nothing but eight cubes put together in a certain way. Thus my structure became more complicated and more interesting because I multiplied my possibilities. One of the works in *Algorithmic Signs*, "P231 C" from 1978 (Fig. 3.7), shows a very successful fourth-dimensional development

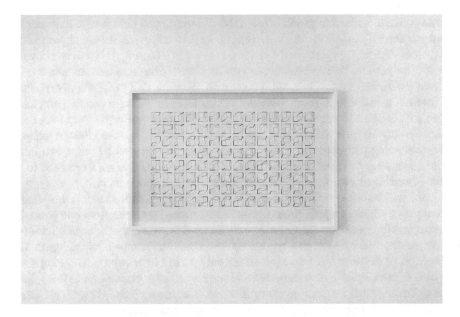

Fig. 3.7 Manfred Mohr, *P-231c*, 1978. ©Manfred Mohr. Image courtesy of the artist

of what I could do by creating an incredible alphabet out of these elements with combinatorial possibilities. Over the years I used higher and higher dimensions for my alphabet, which is nothing else than the systems becoming more complex. And just to clarify the term, I'm not interested in dimensions as a mystical entity. I'm interested in its mathematical definition. And the higher I went in dimensions, the more those elements became a vocabulary for me. The complexity allowed me to invent more and more interesting solutions. In each dimension I asked myself, "What do I want to do in this dimension"? The more possibilities I got by progressing to higher dimensions, the less I was interested in the complete structure, because it occurred to me that it was not the complete structure I wanted to show, but only certain aspects or elements of it.

FF: Why did you choose the cube as your basic element and not, for example, the pyramid, which is based on an even more basic element?

MM: Because the pyramid is not a basic form. You can see from what I just said that I am not really interested in the structure of the cube itself. I'm interested in a basic structure and I play with it, which incidentally is a cube. The more I increased the complexity, the more the cube disappeared in the sense of a visual object and became what I call a "diagonal path", which, as I will show you later, became an even more abstract alphabet that nonetheless still comes from the idea of having an instrument to play with. Even the most complex cube, as, for example, the 100-dimensional cube, is an instrument for me; even though I never show it, because I'm not interested in showing the complete structure itself. I'm only interested in showing aspects of it. I always like to make this parallel with music: in music you have twelve half-tones, but you don't play them all together. You choose this tone or that tone, and you make a melody. In literature we have the same: our alphabet has twenty-six letters, but you don't just print all twenty-six letters to make a book. You choose some letters and make words. Having this in mind, I do exactly the same thing with the hypercube: I invent a word, sort of going through the structure and taking a certain path, and that path is like a word. When I choose that word, or that melody, if you like, that becomes my element with which I work. Once I calculate all these kinds of things, the interesting part occurs in the higher dimension which then I bring down into two dimensions to see what it looks like. It is very important to me to go back to a two-dimensional semiotic sign because that's what I'm interested in.

As I said before, one of my greatest discoveries in my artistic search is the "diagonal path", which is a path through a multidimensional structure from one point to its diagonally opposite point, crossing each dimension once in that structure. It is not a single diagonal between two opposite points, but a very complex line going along the edges of the structure. Choosing a diagonal path in a hypercube and rotating it in n dimensions results in an unexpected and surprising linear element. With this I find semiotic signs that I cannot invent or imagine. You can only find these signs. This becomes an environment so vast that I'm still exploring it today.

FF: In your production, I noticed many sequential drawings, as you call them. How do you describe them?

MM: Let me give you an example. If you draw a house, you draw a house and that's it. But if you want to draw different views of a house, then there are many solutions. In order to show many solutions, you go into a series of developments. It's almost like a movie, but I didn't want to make movies with these sequences, because I did not want to have linear time as an artistic element. I wanted single signs that I could choose to look at forwards and backwards in time whenever I wanted. That's why I drew different developments of the signs. It is a series of stills, a development in time, but as sequential drawings using different generating rules.

FF: I see an analogy with systems art in the way these sequential drawings are made. Do you see any connection with it?

MM: Yes, definitely, it's almost the same thing except—and because of programming—I have a deeper inside knowledge of the possibilities in a system. Most systematic artists have a visual approach to what they can do and are limited to that. I can control something that I don't know in advance what it will look like, and it is possible that it will result in something fantastic and unknown. As I said before, I don't come from a visual approach; I come from a logical approach. It's a different attitude towards the results. The results might look similar, but it's not done from a visual point of view, it's done from a logical point of view, which is reflected in a richer outcome, impossible to achieve otherwise.

FF: I read that in 1973 you published your statement in the Computer Arts Society's bulletin *Page*. Were you in contact with CAS members?

MM: Yes, I met them all in 1970 at the exhibition *Computer Graphic 70*, where I showed my computer drawings for the first time. Some of the pieces that are now in the Victoria & Albert Museum collection are from that show. I edited the bulletin *Page 28* in 1973 as a survey of what was happening in Paris in the computer arts at that time.

FF: Going back to the development of the cube, when you started to work on the 4D hypercube, did you see this as a direct continuation, as a logical consequence, of your research and work?

MM: Yes, absolutely, because I was interested in complexity. I started to work with 4D hypercubes in 1977. If you take two cubes and move them apart and connect all the corresponding vertices with each other, the result is eight interconnected cubes, which is a four-dimensional hypercube. My graphic instrument now becomes eight times more complex. You can go on and do the same procedure with two four-dimensional hypercubes and you will get a structure with forty cubes, a five-dimensional hypercube. If you continue with a six-dimensional hypercube, you will get 160 cubes. If you go on and on, you can reach billions of cubes. The complexity becomes an infinite structure and an absolutely crazy alphabet.

FF: Do you ever feel overwhelmed by this complexity?

MM: Not really. Every time I explore a different dimension I look for what I can do specifically with that complexity. If you look through my work phases, as I went through higher and higher dimensions I always found distinct artistic solutions.

FF: Then you started designing and building small PCs to run your programs. Can you tell me more about it?

MM: I went up and up in complexity, but visually I became more and more minimal, and at one point my drawings were so minimal that I couldn't explain with a straight face that this was complicated.

I consider myself a "maximal minimalist" and ask myself, "How can I convey to somebody the complexity even though it might be only five lines"? I felt that I should go to moving images and colours used as distinctions to get an answer. I wrote a program to rotate my substructures of a hypercube in *n* dimensions and filled certain areas with random colours. With the movement of this structure the multidimensional structure became somehow apparent, not as a real understanding but in a feeling that one could follow this structural movement. The observer has the impression of "feeling" this complex structure without understanding it completely but nevertheless getting a certain satisfaction out of it. The complexity became visual. In order to show these developments on a screen, I wanted to show my work in a specially constructed set-up which then became my artwork itself.

I knew that I had to build a machine by myself. When I was a kid I built radios and amplifiers, so electronics was never foreign to me, but I had never built a computer before.

I got some literature about it and bought a PC and took it completely apart. Then I studied all the pieces and their functions. Once I understood everything, I designed my own computer, bought the parts, and assembled it.

FF: So you started building this because you couldn't find the right technology available?

MM: In the early days (1969) when I dreamed of using a computer in my work to render my thoughts of a generative art I had to find a computer, which I then found at the University of Vincennes and later at the meteorology institute in Paris.

An artist always has to find his tools or invent them. At one point, in 1975, I even modified a plotter by replacing the pen with a steel needle and drew on a copper plate and thus made etchings with the computer. I always try to find a way to express what I want to do, and that includes inventing or modifying a machine. So, going back to the building of a PC, I wanted to build a computer which would be a dedicated tool that only ran my programs in real time as my art. I constantly observe what is happening in technology, but I only use it if I think it will be helpful to me. There is a danger in being obsessed by technology and always wanting to use the latest development. I have a lot of friends who got carried away and lost themselves in all the latest products, and in the end they did nothing artistically. They just played with the latest toys.

FF: When you started developing the programs based on the eleven-dimensional hypercube using the diagonal paths as compositional building blocks, where did you see the composition of your work starting from?

MM: A diagonal path is a construct, which is in itself a logical and mathematical entity. I first used a diagonal path in 1977 with the 4D hypercube and since then I have used this construct frequently. A diagonal path is a line connecting two diagonally opposite points through a dimensional structure. For example, in an 11D hypercube, it passes through each of the eleven dimensions once, and as a result you get a line with eleven segments. Since I cannot imagine how such a line would look in a 2D projection, I have to calculate it first. At this point I make decisions about how I want to proceed and what I want to do with it (Figs. 3.8 and 3.9).

FF: How does this connect to chance in your work?

MM: You can write a logical structure in a program, to make decisions to do either this or that. Most of my programs are based on such logical structures: for example, "Draw a cube". But now comes the next question: "Which rotation should this cube have"? That question is a variable: rotation can be 50 degrees, 20 degrees, or any other angle. You call a random number when there are different possibilities and all have equal value. You use a random number so that the computer can go on calculating because a decision has to be made to continue the flow of the program.

That's called a parameter: at a certain point you can have a random decision because it doesn't change the content but it changes the visuals. My programs are mostly systematic, but once in a while random decisions have to be made. These

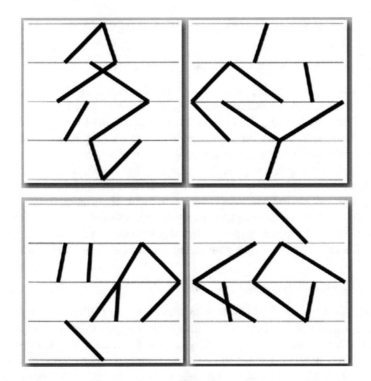

Fig. 3.8 Manfred Mohr, *P-225a*, 1978. ©Manfred Mohr. Image courtesy of the artist

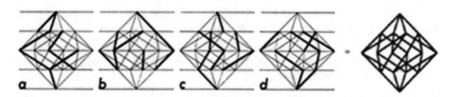

Fig. 3.9 Manfred Mohr's notes showing the graph of the 4D hypercube (32 lines) and how it is randomly divided into 4 parts of 8 lines each. ©Manfred Mohr. Image courtesy of the artist

elements are always in my work. I have programs that are all deterministic, but they are very rare.

FF: So what does randomness give to your work?

MM: It gives solutions one can't think of. Because you're blocked by your own psychology and use certain things in a particular way and not in another way, but the random numbers prevent that. For example, if I didn't like 30-degree angles, I would never draw 30-degree angles. But if 30-degree angles are in the range of angles I allow in a program and a 30-degree angle comes up, it's a relief, because finally I can draw a 30-degree angle. It overcomes my fears and the impossibility of being free.

Randomness can change many things and allows many more possibilities related to one's thinking.

FF: And in terms of coding, what are the foundations of your work?

MM: I started by learning Fortran, and I still write in Fortran. It's like a language. If I want to solve a visual problem I immediately know how to write the code. Programming is a very basic thing. All computer languages do the same thing. Computer languages are hierarchical: on the lowest level you have to write all instructions yourself, and the higher you go the more the computer languages are developed. In a very highly developed computer language like Processing, most of the possible instructions are already written for you. There is no difference between making a drawing with Fortran or with Processing; it will do the same thing. It doesn't matter which language you use. Since I have written thousands of programs in Fortran over the years, I can refer to them and use them, so why should I rewrite every time from scratch. I have a "library" of programs I wrote, and I can refer to them when I need them.

FF: So how would you describe your work?

MM: My work is visual. It can look mathematical, and of course I have to use mathematical elements to do my art. Mathematics in my art is like the "four wheels" of a car. If you want to move the car, you need the wheels, but that doesn't say anything about the car. I don't show the mathematical possibilities of what you can or can't do. There are many artists who show mathematical functions and how they look. I'm not interested in that. I use elements of mathematics to realise my ideas. I do not consider my art as a mathematical art. It is the result of an idea that—independently of its logical content—has to stand alone and defend itself as an independent artistic statement. Mathematicians are not necessarily interested in my work because I'm not proving anything mathematically. I'm using something mathematical to do something visual, which is not their field. I'm doing my work in a scientific way, but I'm not a scientist.

FF: If you could choose three of your works that made you particularly proud of, or happy about, the results, which would you choose?

MM: It's really impossible to choose, like choosing your favourite child. I'm proud of what I have done and not about one single piece. You might think years after you solved a problem that you could have solved it differently, but a few months ago, I went back to an old drawing to see if I could find another solution to that problem and realised that no solution would have been better. It's an intuitive thing, finding the right direction. You make mistakes, of course, and you go back to rethink it. When I look back on what I did, I think most of the time that I found the right solution.

FF: So how do you see the evolution of your work?

MM: I don't see it as a linear evolution. Of course, everything I make builds on the lessons I've learned. Sometimes you gain new knowledge and then you do something you could not have done before. Even though experience is additive in a certain way, it isn't really. As you also change psychologically, there are many things that change. I could not make drawings now in the same way I made them in the 1960s. They would become something else. The curious thing, though, is that, if I drew on a plotter now a program I wrote in 1970, it would reflect my thinking of 1970. If I drew that same program a hundred years from now, it would still be exactly like the drawing I did in 1970 and would still reflect my thinking from 1970. This philosophical dilemma drove me crazy, because in the art market and in art history, this would not be an honest thing to do. This dilemma can be solved by marking clearly the date of creation and the date of execution on an artwork. It's a very modern phenomenon that a logic can be frozen in time and new works produced from this frozen logic forever.

FF: Your early works were mainly black and white and your more recent ones have very vibrant colours. How did colour come into your work?

MM: I started with black and white in 1960 and was convinced—and I even made a bet with my teacher—that anything I wanted to say could be said in the form of yes/no, or, if you want, in black and white with rare exceptions of grey. That was true until the year 1999, when, as I explained to you earlier, I ran into a philosophical problem. I couldn't communicate the complexity of my work, and so I had to find a new way to communicate with the viewer. I came to the conclusion that using random colours as distinctions could show the inherent complexity of the work. On the other hand, I still use black and white. It depends on what I want to say.

FF: It's not because technology did not allow you certain choices …

MM: No. As I said before, technology is something I take only if I need it. I use technology only if my idea requires it. I don't use a new technology just because it's available.

FF: Is there any specific technological tool that you wish existed already but is not yet available?

MM: I know there are technologies that are not available now, but I know they will come sooner or later. For example, I dream of an electronic ink, a liquid you can paint on the wall and it becomes a digital screen. I'm sure it will come, because as soon as a human being can think of something, there will be a day when it will arrive.

FF: This is not something that will end or block or diminish your creativity.

MM: No, because I dream all sorts of things. I would like to create elements that grow on a wall and/or disappear if I want them to. For at least fifty years, I have dreamed of inventing or finding a magnetism related to sound.

FF: How would that work?

MM: Everything in the world is based on frequencies. Certain areas in the frequency band are magnetic, so maybe another part of the vast frequency spectrum can be magnetic also. Maybe one could pull this magnetism into a different frequency band? I had this idea when I lived in Paris in the 1960s. The street outside my apartment was very noisy and I envisioned wired windows that would eat up all the noise and leave the inside completely quiet. New technologies are going in this direction, but not as I envisioned it. Computers are so fast now that you can almost calculate the negation of the sound in real time. The sound and its negative would be able to cancel each other out and there would be no sound left.

FF: In terms of technology and what was available when you started programming, did you find that it was in line with your experimentations or did you feel you needed something more sophisticated?

MM: The technology in the 1960s was very basic. The engineers had just developed a machine that could draw, so I used it. I was always interested in drawing semiotic signs, which are two-dimensional and tell their own story. A plotter was the perfect technology for me. Slowly technology developed in all sorts of directions, but I was not interested in every direction it took. For example, at the beginning I was not interested in colours since I was interested in making "binary drawings" in black and white; colours would have made them more beautiful, but I was not interested in this aspect at that point. The screens as a visual element had not been developed yet; they came much later, and they were incredibly expensive. In the early 1980s, when I applied for a Guggenheim grant to buy that kind of equipment, they wrote back to me saying that they supported art, not technology. So sometimes the technology was too expensive for me to use. But the drawing was always my central point. When I started to work in higher and higher complexities, I understood that to transmit the idea of a multidimensional construct you had to show it in motion. That's when I decided to build screen-based works (2000), which animated these elements in real time, and people started to feel that there was something behind these visuals that held everything together, the logic. I was rather successful with this decision to build screen-based artworks.

FF: What did you feel when you added colour to your constructions? What did colour offer you compared with your previous monochromatic black and white phase?

MM: In the early 1990s, as I said before, the content of my art became very compli-cated, but the visuals were extremely minimal, and I could not easily explain how this minimal information was in reality very complicated. So how could I transmit this idea of an underlying complicated structure, which was not visible? To make this structure somehow visible, I thought that by rotating this structure in n dimen-sions and adding random colours, solely as distinctions, one would see because of the movement that there is a logical element in the work, a coherent structure. In fact, unexpected colour combinations were helpful for the understanding of the spatial relations because the difference in contrasting colours reinforces the spatial relationships. This is what I was interested in.

FF: From what you say about your use of colour, I find the two works on canvas we have exhibited in Venice extremely telling ("P1011_D" of 2004 and "P1011_Ms" of 2004, Figs. 3.3 and 3.4). Can you tell me more about these two works and how they interact with each other?

Figure 3.3. Manfred Mohr, "P1011_D", 2004. ©Manfred Mohr. Image courtesy of the artist.

Figure 3.4. Manfred Mohr, "P1011_Ms", 2004. ©Manfred Mohr. Image courtesy of the artist.

MM: These works represent my research into the eleven-dimensional hypercube. As I mentioned earlier, I was not interested in the complete structure, because in this case there would be 42,240 three-dimensional cubes involved, and the painting would resemble a blackboard. So I chose only a certain number of cubes from the total structure. The sides of those chosen cubes were randomly coloured with black or white by the program. Imagine that you throw hundreds of little cubes in a box and look at them from the top: all the black sides add up to larger forms and all the white sides also add up to larger forms. Where there aren't any cubes on the 2D projection, one could look through the structure and see a green background. This construct is a mathematical structure and therefore is an indivisible unit. When this structure is rotating in eleven dimensions, it stretches, it pulls, it comes towards you or goes away from you, but everything stays mathematically together. The rotation creates unforeseeable images that are complete surprises. To explain the idea of how all the black colour or all the white colour is adding up to create forms—you could compare that to a tree standing in the sunlight and the totality of the leaves adds up to a shadow on the floor. One can say, in this sense, that these paintings show a shadow from the eleventh dimension.

FF: How do you see your work evolving now?

MM: I have no idea. I don't know what I will do tomorrow. I play around, go for a walk. Things come up very unexpectedly, I don't know where they come from—one dreams of something and tries it the next day. Last night I dreamed of a solution for a problem I was trying to solve three days ago. It's a very strange process. There is you and there is your mind, and your mind knows more than you know. Sometimes, if you're doing something but you're not sure of your solution, you sleep on it and the next day you have an answer. It's because your mind works constantly and finds solutions you are not consciously aware of yet.

FF: I agree, we have so many inhibitions …

MM: Yes, but not only that. I think there are two systems, and you can "talk to yourself". The left brain and the right brain are fighting each other because the left brain is the experimental one, it invents crazy things, while the right brain says "No, you're not allowed to do that". They are fighting, and the outcome is that they get together and find a solution.

FF: This is a nice way to describe your work, which has rational and emotional parts combined.

MM: Yes, that's true. I have a funny anecdote about this, which happened at my exhibition in Zurich before I used the computer. At that time I made very precise geometric drawings, but in one drawing I had a part where I made some sort of "romantic" scribbly parallel lines. At the opening, the Swiss painter Richard Lohse, a very rational and strict artist, came up to me and said, "Mr Mohr, you're not allowed to do that"! Referring to the wiggly lines in my drawing. Since then, I always hear his voice when I am doing something not systematic.

FF: Your first show with the computer was in Paris in 1971. How was it received by the critics and by the public?

MM: I had at ARC at the Musée d'Art Moderne de la Ville de Paris the first one-person show of digital art in a museum worldwide. It was quite an event: the television came, the newspapers wrote about it, but in the art magazines there was no mention of it. Art critics were afraid about the connection of computers and art. They didn't know how to write about it and walked away. For years nobody really wanted to write about this type of art. Once in a while there was an article that mentioned the use of the computer in my art. People were largely aggressive to me. I once gave a lecture where I showed my work and they threw raw eggs at me, because they considered the use of computers as bourgeois, or a military machine to kill art, and so on. They kept saying, "That's not art"! But I kept laughing at that, thinking, "Okay, if it is not art, but it is for sure my work".

FF: How did that show come about and did it turn out how you wanted? Were you happy about it?

MM: Yes, definitely. At that time I did some work for the artist Ruth Francken, building electronic devices for her art installations where you could press a button to play music. She knew the director of ARC at the museum in Paris, Pierre Gaudibert, and told him about my artwork with the computer. He was very interested in my ideas and came to the meteorology institute to see what I was doing. He offered to organise a show and we selected the works together and installed the show. He was never negative about this kind of approach to art. He was convinced that this was something worth supporting.

The director of the museum, André Berne-Joffroy, wrote a critical essay in the catalogue and was very supportive too. But the general art world looked the other way. Even today, sometimes if I show my drawings to some people and say that they are made by the computer, I still get this strange look. People are still reluctant to accept that there is computer-based art.

FF: Have you noticed a change of attitude in the art world?

MM: Yes, especially since 1982, when the personal computer came on the market, disbelief has changed to interest. With the introduction of Photoshop, vector graphics was pushed aside in favour of raster graphics, a completely different expression. Programming suddenly meant something completely different. From computer art it became digital art. Digital art started when people understood that photos are made of dots, and dots can be calculated, so suddenly the world woke up to digital art. The art world was open to digital art because it was very easy to play with these programs. For example, one could distort a face, make it long or short. The computer thus became more a part of daily life, and now they are everywhere, so using computers changed from an exercise in programming into gaming. Computers got integrated into daily life and there is no longer aggression towards them. It's only when you go back to actual programming, some people still say, "This is not done by hand". But digital art is accepted everywhere.

FF: In terms of digital conservation, what are the most important issues for you to consider?

MM: I know about the problems, but I'm not particularly interested in them. I give instructions on how to repair my screen-based works, how to do certain things, and what to watch for. I'm not interested in reconstructing things. If a digital print has a scratch, that's ageing. If a museum wants to reinstall a program, they have all the instructions. I give all the information I have about my work, but I'm not too concerned about the conservation aspects; they have to figure out for themselves what to do. If somebody buys a screen-based work of mine, in twenty years they have to rebuild it, but that should not be a problem. New problems occur, but they can be solved. If you have a magnetic video tape you have to rewrite it every few years because magnetism gets destroyed over time. Years ago, a computer program was written on punched cards, but there is no machine to read them today. If the code was written on a computer magnetic tape, you would have the same problem. Conservation is a big problem, but over time people learn how to deal with it.

FF: So in the instructions that you give …

MM: My instructions take many forms. There is the program, which can always be rewritten in another language if one needs to. I also give instructions on how I built the machines physically and I also supply drawings, so they have visual instructions. I have a list of things that can go wrong and solutions to them. I give them the manuals, but there is always some external problem. At the beginning I used to give instructions on a CD, but now nobody has a reader for that either. Lately I've given my instructions on memory sticks, but in twenty years they will be obsolete as well. There is no end to it. Years ago, when I was still painting, I had to give collectors a list of the paints I used, which is in a way the same thing but much simpler.

FF: We just had the honour of exhibiting your work at the Bevilacqua La Masa Foundation, in St Mark's Square, Venice. Can you tell me how you feel about exhibiting your art in such a traditional environment?

MM: It feels fantastic. The building is beautiful, the rooms and the show are fantastic. And I find that the space, its quietness, are adequate to what we are doing, because our work needs to be shown in a way that people can contemplate it. The work that we, all five artists, are doing is very contemplative. I've been showing my work in many different places, but this is the first time I've exhibited in Venice and it's great to be here—and I hope the water doesn't rise too much!

FF: Actually, the water enhances this sense of tranquility and meditation.

MM: That's very true. The fact that there are no cars, no sounds from the traffic, the first thing that I noticed when coming to Venice was its quietness, and this makes it a fantastic place for this exhibition.

This interview clarifies how the discovery of computer programming and logic applied to art became the foundations of Mohr's creativity and art practice. Two key steps that helped Mohr in achieving this were the realisation, coming from the understanding of Max Bense's philosophy, that his art could be rationally constructed; the second step, inspired by Pierre Barbaud's computational programmed music, was the understanding that through computer programming one could apply a logic procedure that creates a rational art. This allowed the artist to create not just a single visual image, but a process that generates many outputs. Both lessons were a revelation for Mohr, who has been and still is surprised by the variety of possibilities produced by a single algorithm and by the role that logic plays in his art practice.

The other key aspect that has emerged from this interview is the importance Mohr has placed in exploring complexity, and how that has been facilitated by learning computer programming and applying it to his art practice. In Mohr, complexity is understood as an infinite structure that creates an alphabet used by the artist to create his own language. It is fascinating to see how this language has allowed the artist to explore creativity for over fifty years, and how this notion still informs his current practice.

The following photos are of artwork on display at the exhibition, the figure number refers to the number on the map of the floor plan of exhibition which can be viewed in Chap. 7.

1. Manfred Mohr, *P-499-Al*, 1993, painted steel, 15 parts, 250 × 1200 cm

2. Manfred Mohr, *P1273_6351*, 2008, pigments, ink on canvas, 90 × 90 cm

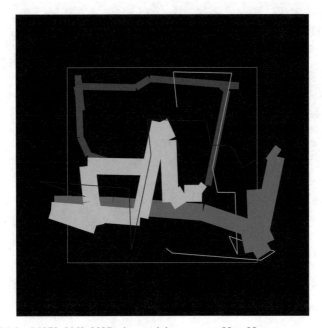

3. Manfred Mohr, *P1273_9168*, 2007, pigment ink on canvas, 90 × 90 cm

5. Manfred Mohr, *P-196-A*, 1977, plotter drawing on paper, 50 × 50 cm

6. Manfred Mohr, *P1622-G*, 2012–14, LCD screen Mac Mini, 45 × 45 × 11 cm

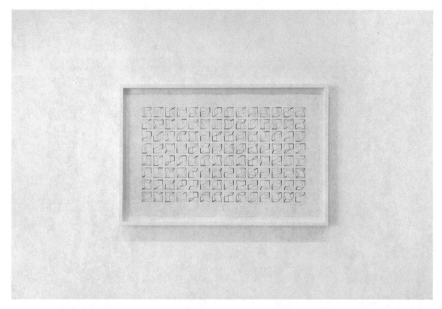

7. Manfred Mohr, *P-231-C*, 1978, plotter drawing on paper, 51 × 82 cm

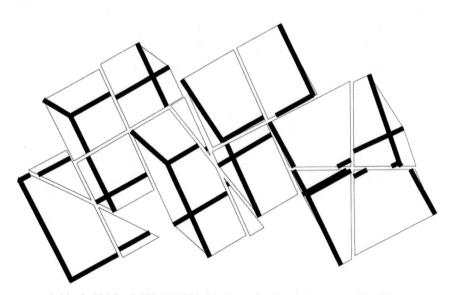

8. Manfred Mohr, *P-370-AZ*, 1984–85, plotter drawing, ink on paper, 65 × 92 cm

9. Manfred Mohr, *P2210-C LCD*, 2015, screen MacMini, 37 × 63 × 11 cm

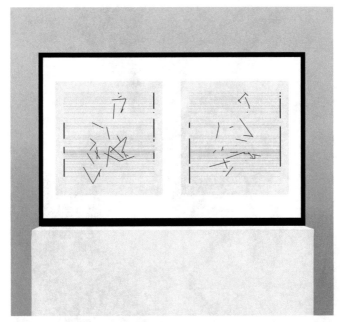

10. Manfred Mohr, *P1680-C*, 2015, LCD screen MacMini, 37 × 63 × 11 cm

11. Manfred Mohr, *P1011_D*, 2004, pigment ink on canvas, 112 × 112 cm

12. Manfred Mohr, *P1011_Ms*, 2004, pigment ink on canvas, 112 × 112 cm

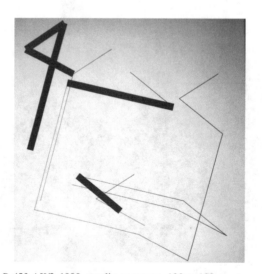

13. Manfred Mohr, *P-453-AK/2*, 1990, acrylic on canvas, 120 × 120 cm

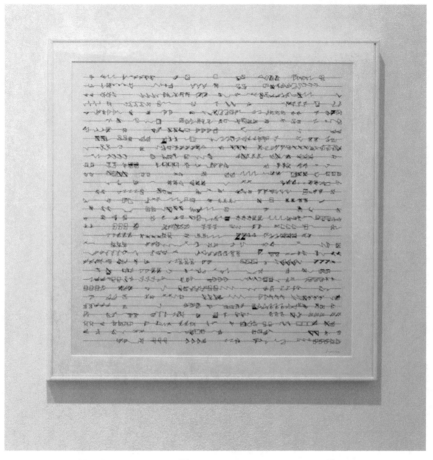

14. Manfred Mohr, *P-021*, 1970, plotter drawing on paper, 52 × 52 cm

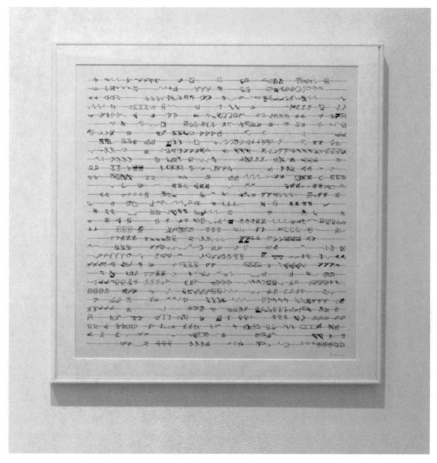

15. Manfred Mohr, *P-036*, 1970, plotter drawing on paper, 52 × 52 cm

16. Manfred Mohr, *P-122*, 1970, plotter drawing on paper, 52 × 52 cm

Further Reading

Manfred Mohr, Artist's Statement, Paris, 1971, in Catalog "Manfred Mohr Computer Graphics -
    Une Esthétique Programmée", ARC - Musée d'Art Moderne de la Ville de Paris, 1971.
Manfred Mohr, Generative Art, in Linda Candy and Ernest Edmonds (eds.), Explorations in Art
    and Technology, Springer-Verlag London 2002, pp. 111–114.
Manfred Mohr, Margit Rosen and Demian Bern (eds.), Der Algorithmus des Manfred Mohr. Texte
    1963–1979. Spector Books, 2014.

Chapter 4
Interview with Vera Molnar

Interview Recorded in Paris, 19 April and 29 May 2017

Vera Molnar was born 1924 in Budapest. She lives and works in Paris. From 1942 to 1947 she studied painting and obtained a diploma in art history and aesthetics from the Budapest College of Fine Arts. In 1946 she created her first non-representational, abstract images. A year later she won a fellowship at the Villa Giulia, Rome, that allowed her to continue her studies in the fine arts. She then moved to France and, from 1947 to 1960, she had the opportunity to work and collaborate with François Molnár, her future husband. From 1959 to 1960 she worked on the "Machine Imaginaire" and in the early 1960s became a cofounder of several artists groups, including the Groupe de Recherche d'Art Visuel (GRAV), who investigated collaborative approaches to mechanical and kinetic art, and "Art et Informatique", a group focused on art and computing. She first exhibited her work in *Konkrete Kunst* (*Concrete Art*), an exhibition organised by her friend Max Bill in Zürich.

In the late 1960s she gained access to a computer at a research lab in Paris and began learning programming languages such as Fortran and Basic. In 1968 she started to create computer-based plotter drawings and algorithmic paintings based on simple geometrical themes.

In 1976, with her husband, she developed the computer software program "Molnárt", and in the same year she exhibited her work in *Transformation* at London Polytechnic. In 1979 she worked at the Atelier de Recherche des Techniques Avancées (ARTA) within the Centre Georges Pompidou in Paris.

In the early 1980s, Molnar became a member of the Centre de Recherche Expérimentale et Informatique des Arts Visuels (CREIAV) at the Sorbonne, Université de Paris I, and her first artist's book, *1% de désordre*, was published. Since the 1990s, her work has been featured in major international solo and group exhibitions, including *Vera Molnar. Lignes, Formes, Couleurs* at the Vasarely Muzeum, Budapest (1990); *De l'esprit à l'œuvre* at the Musée d'Art et d'Histoire, Cholet (1995); *Extrait de 100.000 milliards de lignes* at the Centre de Recherche, d'Échange et de Diffusion pour l'Art Contemporain (Crédac), Ivry-sur-Seine (1999); and *Thèmes et variations* at the Musée des Beaux Arts, Brest (2005).

© Springer Nature Switzerland AG 2022
F. Franco, *The Algorithmic Dimension*, Springer Series on Cultural Computing,
https://doi.org/10.1007/978-3-319-61167-9_4

In 2005 she was the recipient of the first lifetime achievement award "d.velop digital art award [ddaa]". In 2018 she won the AWARE Outstanding Merit Award (AWARE *Prix d'Honneur*), an award supported by the French Ministry of Culture that acknowledges leading female figures in the world of culture.

Francesca Franco: Unlike many of your colleagues who pioneered the field of computational art starting from a mathematical, scientific or engineering background, you are one of the few who were initially trained in the Fine Arts. How did you start using a computer to make art?

Vera Molnar: I had this idea for a long time but at that point the computer was not available to everybody and was very expensive. So I started working with a method that I named "The Machine Imaginaire" ("The Imaginary Machine/Computer"). But the first opportunity that I had to work on a computer, albeit briefly, was in 1968, first with Honeywell Bull and later at the Centre de Calcule Universitaire.

FF: What made you switch to the computer? What made you think "OK, from now on I'm going to make art by programming the computer"?

VM: It happened step by step. First, with Honeywell Bull, you had to imagine something and it was translated into numbers, 0100101, etc., and you had to imagine how it would look. It was not very easy, but I was persistent, and tried again and again. The big change in my life happened when I got in touch with the Centre de Calcule at Orsay, when the screen appeared. At the beginning there were no screens, so you had to work with the supposition that what you are imagining will come out on paper, but that was not always the case. I remember very well when the computer with a screen arrived; I had the impression it had been invented especially for me, not for all those people working in science!

FF: And you were one of the very few female artists working with a computer at that time … Did you know other female artists who were using computers at that time?

VM: There were some. I met Lillian Schwartz, Grace Hertlein, and in France I remember there was the girlfriend of Hervé Huitric, Monique Nahas.

FF: Your work is based on a series of variations that are programmed works that you then select. How does the selection process work for you?

VM: Three things: one is my personal taste, what I personally like when it is hung on a wall; secondly, if it is exactly what I imagined in my head; and third, if it is the contrary, if there is a surprise, something that I had not imagined. The fantastic feature of computer art is that you can try things which are exactly what you had in your mind but you can change them. It remains your idea but there is something new in it. This is fascinating, the surprise!

FF: What was the biggest surprise that you had when you started working on computers in 1968?

VM: For me it was the fact that when I began to work with computers, there was no screen. One of the biggest emotions of my life was when the screen appeared, since you had an immediate response to your input, and this was fantastic! You could change something, and this would appear either as something you imagined, or something else, or something between the two. It was an amusing life!

FF: Of the five artists featuring in *Algorithmic Signs* in Venice, Manfred Mohr is the one you have known for the longest time. Can you tell me your memories about meeting him?

VM: It was a very amusing thing. It was in Paris around 1968, during the student revolution. I remember it was the first time I was invited to speak about art and the computer, at the University of Vincennes, just outside Paris, the first university in France where you could go without the baccalaureate degree—it was very democratic! I was invited by Frank Popper to speak about my work. I arrived in the big lecture room and I saw not thirty students, but sixty shoes in front of me! As a sign of protest, they had all put their feet up on the tables. I was so astonished! But there was only one man who didn't put his feet up on the table: it was Manfred Mohr. I then got to know him well and a few years later, in 1971, I went to see his show at the Musée d'Art Moderne in Paris.

FF: Do you see any differences between your work and that of your colleagues?

VM: I think one difference is the background from where you are coming, if you are a mathematician, a scientist, or an artist … it changes your way of thinking. And today it is the same thing. I think it was Renoir or Monet who once said that painting must be a feast for the eyes. It is not my *motto* but something like that is in my head.

FF: I understand many of your works are inspired by nature. So where does your inspiration come from?

VM: You see, in life I get inspired by what surrounds me, the nature around you but also the ateliers of my friends, visiting museums, all of it. Of course I come often to nature, as you can see in my *cahiers* for example. Sometimes I start from a pure random image, like this image of a bush in the moonlight (Fig. 4.1); and I work out how to make very complicated images in one line [Note: she tries to depict the complexity of the bush by using a single line that never stops with the pen that never lifts from the paper] and after that I told myself how it can look like a combination of this disorder of lines and one geometric form, and I tried with a square. That was my first idea; it was not very convincing. After that, I tried with a circle [Note: the moon in the picture], and I liked it more.

FF: So was this process to make the bush in your drawing programmed from the beginning?

VM: Yes, this was programmed, but it also surprised me. I like to combine things that are not supposed to be brought together. I like impossible situations, chaos of lines and circles … I've been trying to combine impossible things together. For example, this work [Note: the image of the bush] was developed with the use of the computer just as a single line that was a separate concept and, when I got that, I wanted to combine it with a geometric form, trying with different forms. I've tried with a square,

Fig. 4.1 Vera Molnar
showing one of her
sketchbooks in her studio,
Paris, 2017. ©Francesca
Franco

with circles. I initially create these ideas in my sketchbook, so this drawing started
as a sketch, but then I made some versions which were bigger and cleaner.

FF: Does your work always start from a sketch?

VM: Yes, and I feel the sketches in my journals are more important than the actual
works. I sketch all the time, wherever I am, like in a café or on the train, so as soon
as I see something in my head, I immediately draw it in the sketchbook. I live with
my colour pencils in my bag …

FF: So those are the first moments where your idea goes onto paper?

VM: Yes, and later I make the bigger works.

FF: So when do you decide whether a certain work will be made into a larger work?
How do you choose the materials that will make the actual work?

VM: That is a very good question! I have at some moment the idea that this is the
best work I've done and I have to sell it, but on looking at my journal later I find
sketches that I never made into artworks and sometimes these projects were more

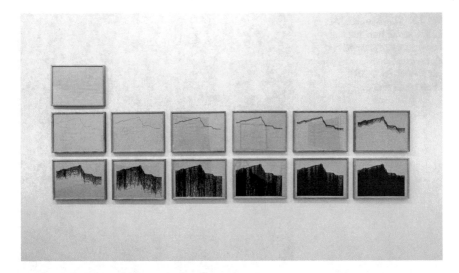

Fig. 4.2 Vera Molnar, *Variations St. Victoire, series No. 0–12*, 1989–1996. ©Vera Molnar. Image courtesy of Giorgio Bombieri

interesting than those which were brought to the state of finished artworks … I have an idea which I want to realise and after that something surprising should emerge as a result of its execution …

FF: And can you tell me more about your choice of colours?

VM: I choose them, but it depends also on the manufacturers and what colours are available for a specific purpose. Colours in my work are not really experimental, lines are. When I was young I was "dure et pure". I was such an absolute extremist, and I wanted to understand everything about art, what makes art. Now I am less and less convinced about that. When I was sixteen, I was so confident about myself that I decided I will be not the Leonardo da Vinci, but the "Leonarda da Budapest"! There was a long series of disappointments, but I have the feeling that I went from one failure to a better one[1] … It is paradoxical, every day at the end of the day I have the impression I didn't understand a thing about what I've done that day, but when I finally look at what I have done in the long run, I have the impression that I made some progress.

FF: In Venice we had the privilege of being able to exhibit one of your works inspired by Cézanne's "Mont Sainte-Victoire" (Fig. 4.2). How did that idea come about?

VM: That was a funny story. I was in the States, my husband had to work in a laboratory and I had plenty of time for myself. I went to the library, and at that time I felt a bit tired about classical regular geometry, squares, circles, triangles, etc., and

---

[1] The artist's statement here is redolent of Beckett's "Ever tried. Ever failed. No matter. Try again. Fail again. Fail better".

Fig. 4.3 Vera Molnar, "Six million seven hundred and sixty-five thousand and two hundred and one Sainte-Victoire", 2012. ©Francesca Franco

in a scientific book I found something I liked. It was the Gaussian curve, which interested me a lot. After that I made many study variations on this curve of Gauss. The last day in the States, all the work done by my husband François and by me was stolen—I was furious, two months of work lost!—I was so upset that I said to myself that I would never do any more work on the curve of Gauss! Twenty years later, I had an exhibition in Aix, the city of Cézanne, and the morning I opened my window, I saw my curve of Gauss: it was the Mont Sainte-Victoire! I changed my mind and began working again on that. I didn't have all the studies I'd made in the States because they had been stolen, but I could remember them. All the studies I had made on the curve of Gauss looked like the Mont Sainte-Victoire! So I got back to that work and made many variations based on that curve (Fig. 4.3).

FF: I'm fascinated by the fact you made several variations of that curve. Variations are the base of most of your work. Can you tell me more about it?

VM: Yes, the purpose of my work is about not being content with one solution but trying to combine things and make discoveries, thereby creating a surprise. It is the purpose of my life to create surprises, for myself first of all.

FF: In your variations, do you see any connection with music?

VM: Yes, I see a special connection. I see the movements of my work and their complexities as being like the "Goldberg Variations" by Bach. They are a portrait of my mind, and I like to see them all together as one piece.

As for the variations on Mont Sainte-Victoire, at one point I decided to make this series of variations starting using only one line, then multiplying it to two, then four, eight, sixteen, and created the work which you have selected to exhibit in Venice. I worked again on this problem very recently. These are some recent developments (Fig. 4.4). They are nine squares, depicting the outline of the mountain in three separate rows, and they are made on nine separate canvases. I have used three different techniques or styles to differentiate them: lines, dots and grey. The "ordered" version shows the three versions like this (Figs. 4.5, 4.6, 4.7 and 4.8). But my idea is that I intend to make nine little pieces of canvas and interchange them, modifying the order of each canvas in the sequence in order to disrupt the initial image. So if somebody buys it, this person has to sign a declaration for me that at least once a month he/she will change the order of the canvases.

FF: What do you see as a *trait d'union* of your work?

VM: Research and curiosity. I'm always curious to see what would happen if I change a colour, or a line …

FF: So is what you get from your programmed works mostly unexpected?

VM: It's a curious combination of the expected and the not expected. The non-expected is very important, but there is a curious equilibrium between randomness and my ideas, between order and disorder, as in all aspects of life (Fig. 4.9).

Molnar's search for a logic system that would generate new images, which started in the late 1940s–early 1950s when Molnar's work was primarily based on abstraction and geometry, took a new turn when she approached chance as a rule that governs the composition of shapes and colours in her work.

As in Manfred Mohr's case, from the late 1960s Molnar has applied a logic procedure and a set of generative rules encoded in algorithms to her compositions, which were executed by a computer. Learning programming languages such as Fortran and Basic, and applying them in the creative process, allowed Molnar to create computer-generated graphics in ink on paper and algorithmic paintings based on simple combinations of lines or geometric shapes such as squares and rectangles that have helped maintaining a link that connects her work to that of her great inspirations, such as Cézanne just to name one of them.

Since the moment Molnar started to develop computer software programs and applied it to her compositions, she has maintained a dynamic dialogue between her manual production and her automated practice, relying on the computer as a tool to perform complex and laborious tasks.

Curiosity and surprise are a constant source of inspiration for Molnar. They still motivate her to explore new paths and produce new work, and represent two key factors motivating us to experience and enjoy Molnar's remarkably powerful production.

Fig. 4.4 Vera Molnar, "Sainte-Victoire Interchangeables (Orange & Blue)", 2017. ©Francesca Franco

Fig. 4.5 Vera Molnar showing the initial sketches of "Sainte-Victoire Interchangeables" in her studio in Paris, 2017. ©Francesca Franco

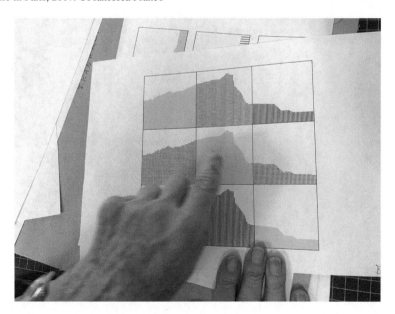

Fig. 4.6 Vera Molnar showing the initial sketches of "Sainte-Victoire Interchangeables" in her studio in Paris, 2017. ©Francesca Franco

Fig. 4.7 Vera Molnar showing the initial sketches of "Sainte-Victoire Interchangeables" in her studio in Paris, 2017. ©Francesca Franco

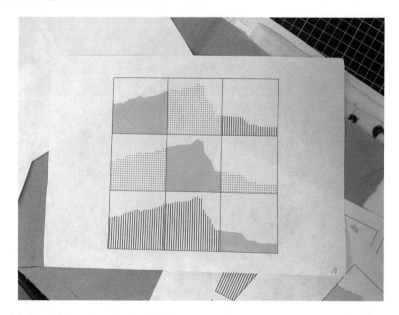

Fig. 4.8 Vera Molnar showing the initial sketches of "Sainte-Victoire Interchangeables" in her studio in Paris, 2017. ©Francesca Franco

Fig. 4.9 Vera Molnar talking about her work in her studio in Paris, 2017. ©Francesca Franco

The following photos are of artwork on display at the exhibition, the figure number refers to the number on the map of the floor plan of exhibition which can be viewed in Chap. 7.

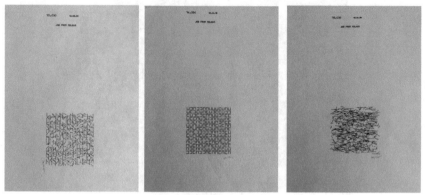

17. Vera Molnar, *Untitled*, 1974–1975, plotter drawings, 36 × 55 cm

18. Vera Molnar, *Series Interruptions*, 1968, plotter drawing, 35 × 35 cm

19. Vera Molnar, *Lettres De Ma Mère*, 1983, plotter drawing, 29 × 25 cm

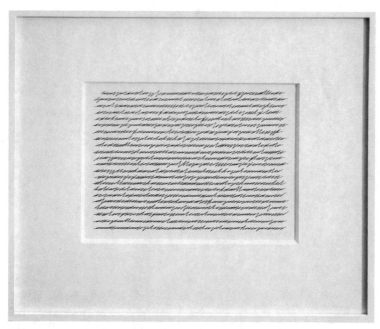

20. Vera Molnar, *Lettres De Ma Mère*, 1983, plotter drawing, 22 × 29 cm

21. Vera Molnar, *Lettres De Ma Mère*, 1983, plotter drawing, 20 × 36 cm

22. Vera Molnar, *Untitled*, 1983, plotter drawing, 32 × 33 cm

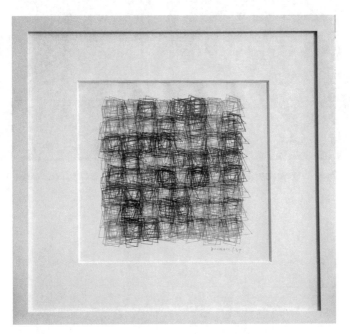

23. Vera Molnar, *Structure De Quadrilateres*, 1983, plotter drawing, 28 × 29 cm

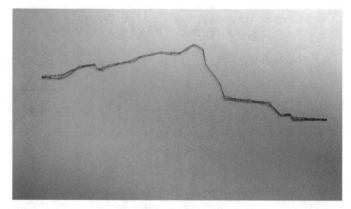

24. Vera Molnar, *Installation based on 13 Variations Mount St. Victoire series*, nails and wool thread, 280 × 80 cm

25. Vera Molnar, *13 Variations Mount St. Victoire series*, 1989–96, laserprint on paper, 31 × 43 cm each

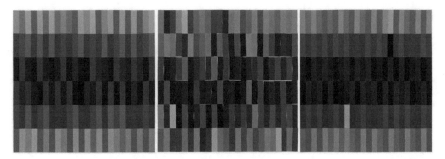

26. Vera Molnar, *144 Rectangles*, 1969, collage, 59 × 179 cm

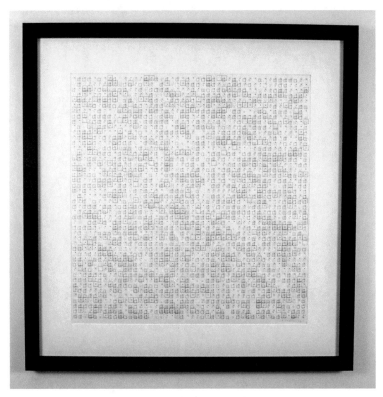

27. Vera Molnar, *Untitled*, 1974, plotter drawing, 97 × 98 cm

Further Reading

Vera Molnar, Description du programme "Molnart" (1974–1976), 1976. Available online at http://www.veramolnar.com/blog/wp-content/uploads/VM1976_molnart.pdf.

Vera Molnar, Un moment éphémère de certitude, 1980. Available online at http://www.veramolnar.com/blog/wp-content/uploads/VM1980_moment.pdf.

Vera Molnar, "Regards sur mes images", in Revue d'Esthétique, No. 7, 1984. Available online at http://www.veramolnar.com/blog/wp-content/uploads/VM1984_regards.pdf.

Chapter 5
Interview with Frieder Nake

Interview Recorded in Bremen, 7 March 2017, and Venice, 20 October 2017

Frieder Nake (b. 1938) is one of the founding fathers of computer art. He produced his first computer-generated artworks in 1963. His first plotted drawings were exhibited at the Galerie Wendelin Niedlich in Stuttgart in November 1965. His most celebrated works include "compArt ER56" (1963–65), "Walk-through-raster" (1966), "Matrix Multiplication" (1967–68), and "Generative aesthetics I" (1968–69). In 1971, he published a provocative article titled "There should be no computer art" (Nake 1971), where he declared his intention of not making computer art anymore. His reasons, as he pointed out, were mainly political: he did not see how he could actively contribute to computer art and, at the same time, be a political activist against Capitalism. He resumed making computational art in the mid-1980s, following the breakdown of the Radical Left. In 1999, with the beginning of his project "CompArt: a space for computer art", Nake returned to his roots as a theoretician, writer, creator and teacher in the domain of digital art. Nake is Professor of Computer Science at the University of Bremen, Germany and Head of CompArt (the Centre of Excellence Digital Art). His teaching and research activities are focussed on computer graphics, digital media, computer art, design of interactive systems, computational semiotics and general theory.

Francesca Franco: In your lectures and writing, you often mention Sol Lewitt and Max Bense's work and how they "played the role of a manifesto" in twentieth-century art (Nake 2010). In particular, you suggest how Bense's "Projects of generative aesthetics" (Bense 1965) could be considered as a computer art manifesto. As an artist, did you feel the need of a manifesto when you started to make art in the early 1960s?

Frieder Nake: If I remember correctly, I didn't feel a need then. I do not recall when I started to try and better understand Max Bense's text "Generative aesthetics"—that was published in German on the occasion of George Nees' first computer art exhibition in the world—so, when did I start to consider that text—which is not written as a manifesto—to be THE manifesto of computer art? It was long after the exhibition of 1965, maybe twenty years after that, in the mid-1980s. I didn't feel

© Springer Nature Switzerland AG 2022
F. Franco, *The Algorithmic Dimension*, Springer Series on Cultural Computing,
https://doi.org/10.1007/978-3-319-61167-9_5

the need of a manifesto, not at all. However, in my archives, there are some of my writings, written on the typical computer printer paper that was used at that time, in the form of sentences that you could easily interpret as "Nake's Manifestos". They are from 1964 if I remember correctly. I didn't feel the need of a manifesto, but maybe I've done something like this.

FF: What were the main points of "Nake's Manifestos"?

FN: They were naïve, something like "We now calculate the images (instead of painting them)", and similar …

FF: Thinking of Max Bense and his *Information Aesthetics* concept, he often talks about artificial art implying the role of artificial intelligence in the production of an artwork, but I understand your take was quite different …

FN: I can tell you a little anecdote about how the term "artificial art" was coined. Bense was fascinated by the world of artificiality, in general. The technical world, and the human in the technical world—these were important topics in his philosophy. The technical world to him is, first of all, artificial in all its facets; and second, it is fragile. The more technology advances, the more fragile it becomes. Fragile in the sense that there is a danger of anything technological breaking down everywhere and always. So computer art, as it was called, constituted a break into visual art by technological means, and that was a triumph, in Bense's view, of the rational over the emotional. At the opening of the first exhibition, on the 4 February 1965, Georg Nees talked briefly about how he made the machine to draw. After he had ended, one of the professors from the fine arts school raised his hand and said "It is very nice what you told us, young man. But tell me, could you make your computer paint the way I do it"? Nees ponders for a moment and then comes up with a fantastic and ingenious answer by saying "Oh, yes, of course, I can do this—under one condition: you must tell me how you do it yourself"! What he says is this: if you know exactly, and can explicitly tell me, how you paint, then I can, of course, write a program. But he may have thought by himself: I bet you do not know how you paint, you just do it. In reacting to this daring answer by Nees, that the artists took almost as an insult, the artists present in the gallery shout at him, leave the place, slam the doors. Bense runs after them begging "Please, gentlemen, stay, this is only *artificial* art". The event took place in 1965. Artificial Intelligence is at one of its early heights. Bense knows about artificial intelligence because of his interest in artificiality, and therefore that word must have sprung up as a spontaneous idea: this is artificial art … the machine is between the artist and the work.

FF: So what were the most inspiring concepts that you drew from Bense?

FN: It was his radical rationalism. During all of my years as a student, I attended Bense's Monday evening lectures, as many intellectuals did in Stuttgart, and I was always fascinated by him. Because his behaviour was totally different from all the other professors I knew, totally different, always provoking. In my memory, I did not understand a word of what he said, but I kept taking notes, and wrote, and wrote; it was fascinating but too complicated for me to grasp, at least this is so in my memory.

However, I do know that I learnt from him about semiotics, and this has stayed with me through all the time. Later on, I figured out that he was much too formal in his account of Peirce's semiotics, but he was the first to tell us about Charles Sanders Peirce and his "theory of signs". Peirce's semiotics was the right one for our time, and he was absolutely correct and right. From my later understanding of semiotics, Bense's interpretation was rather shallow. He formalised it rigorously whereas, from my understanding, Peirce would not have formalised semiotics.

FF: So what has semiotics taught you?

FN: I have learned that the work of art is a sign, and you can approach everything in art from a semiotic point of view. Ever since, I have always taken this perspective. Each of my programs starts from a basic repertoire of signs that are needed to do anything; there must also be available transformations of a semiotic kind that are to be applied to the basic signs, but also to the already-derived new signs.

FF: Can you give me a practical example, using your work, where you applied these concepts?

FN: Well, let us take a very simple one (simple in terms of their visual complexity), let us take a polygon. A polygon is a straight line segment, followed by another straight line segment, followed by yet another one, and so on, hundreds or thousands of straight line pieces (edges). Wherever one of the segments ends, it takes a bend and continues in the new direction for a short or long distance. That is all that is needed to make a polygon. Now, to write a program creating such polygons is trivial. When you do it, the running program will create polygons, one after the other. They may all have the same number of edges, or the number of edges varies from one to the next, perhaps randomly. What you see as the human perceiver is not those edges, at least if the image is complex enough. You don't really see those edges. You see a figure as a chaotic *Gestalt*. Of course, you may become aware of what the polygon is made up of. You may react by saying "Oh yes, I see this one line that is continued—but is this here now a new line or still the old one"? Complexity quickly goes beyond what you can still distinguish. Here we get at the point where, against all its simplicity, I can say why I use this simple case. The short straight line segments, the edges of the polygon, of which I know they are there, because I have programmed the simple drawing—they are the elements out of which something more complex emerges. We see this, but we know that it is not explicitly built into the program. What we see is more than is in the program. The program only deals with the basic signs, the edges. But then those edges are criss-crossing and intersecting here and there; they build little heaps here, that are not in the program; they emerge from the elementary repertoire of signs, creating new signs that come as a potential with the elementary repertoire.

FF: So can this be applied, for instance, to your "Matrix Multiplication works" (Fig. 5.1)?

FN: Yes, it can, in general and with certain adjustments in detail. It is in fact almost trivial, because the complexity in the matrix multiplications is with the mathematics.

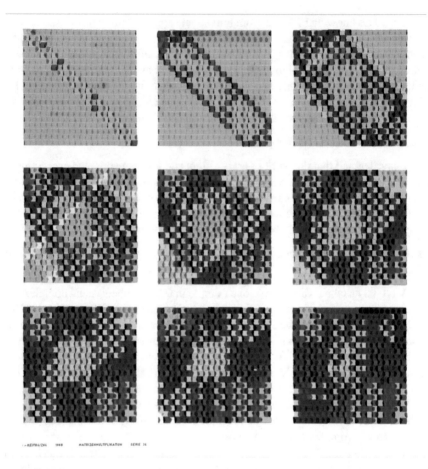

Fig. 5.1 Frieder Nake, *Matrix Multiplication series 34*, 1968. ©Frieder Nake. Courtesy of the artist

I don't want to go into mathematical details here, so it should suffice to say that this work starts from a case of a specific kind of matrices. They are called stochastic matrices. Each of their rows is a sequence of numbers, all between 0 and 1, and such that they sum up to 1. I take one of those, actually randomly chosen, and multiply it by itself. The result is again multiplied by the first matrix, and so on. In this way I construct the sequence of the powers of the original matrix. But where and how does the graphic image appear? It appears as a visualisation of one or the other of those powers of the given stochastic matrix. More precisely: once in a while, the current state of the matrix-products is selected to be transformed into a coloured square. How is this done? Since all the numbers in the matrix are between 0 and 1, I divide the interval [0, 1] into as many subintervals as I want to use colours. To each of the subintervals a colour is assigned. So now, looking through the matrix element by element, I get a colour assigned to each number. Each of those colours then becomes the colour of a small square (whose size is a parameter of the program). That small square is automatically coloured by its uniquely determined colour.—To summarise what is happening here, we see this: a sequence of the powers of a stochastic matrix is calculated, and by virtue of a correspondence of numbers and colours, once in a while the current state of the sequence of matrices is transformed into a coloured square of little squares. A mathematical process is transformed into a process of coloured squares.—We see a mathematical theorem at work here. What we see on screen, I call the *surface*. What we do not see is the process of the multiplications. This hidden level, I call the *subface*. Surface and subface, in computing, belong together inseparably. One depends on the other, and only together do they make sense. This duplication is essential to the entire world of computing. The fact that signs are relations, not things, appears here in a specific form. The "sign" topic, the semiotics of the situation, here appears in a double sense: there is a hidden mathematics, a world where the signs are numbers—and intervals, by the way; on the other hand, there is a visible world where the signs are those little coloured squares. The entire procedure makes sense only when you take into account a mathematical theorem behind the scene. This mathematical theorem is responsible for the gradual transformation of a rather chaotic arrangement of colours in bright yellow into columns of squares that are getting more and more constant in colours. Our conjecture may be that there must be a law behind what is happening.

FF: Is this something that you set up at the very beginning when writing the algorithm? And if so, what was the statement in this particular case?

FN: Correct is that I set up the association of colours with ranges of numbers. What I did not set up is the theorem. If the original matrix is a stochastic one—as I have indicated before—I can predict that the process of multiplying over and over again will lead to the gradual appearance of those columns that don't change anymore. The original chaos is forced into a more and more orderly appearance. That's a consequence of the hidden mathematics behind the scene.

FF: Is there an element of randomness here?

FN: There is randomness in the choice of the first matrix. After this original choice within limits, it's all mathematics. Of course, there are different ways for the program to choose the first matrix. I might say "Put nonzero numbers only into the diagonal, or smear them around, or do something else to the form of the original matrix …".

FF: So what is the most exciting aspect of this work from your perspective?

FN: The excitement here is to observe how, from a more or less chaotic origin, you get a gradual process of order building up. As if there were a geometric order behind the curtain that has to be released.

FF: So do you see this geometric structure, this system that you use to create these images, as an organising principle for your works?

FN: Yes, in some way. In the particular case of building the powers of those stochastic matrices, the resulting matrix more and more approaches a limit state. In the visual transformation this shows as the appearance of the constantly looking columns. They mean that something is happening in the same way independent of the situation at the start. In the long run, this tells us, a system of this kind will always behave the same way.

FF: So you start with an algorithm, or procedure, and then you let the computer run. How does that work, for example, in "Matrix Multiplications"?

FN: In our example of "Matrix Multiplications", the algorithm is doing nothing but build the next power of the matrix, and once in a while transforms it into the associated colours. I wrote this program in 1967. I presented results of it at an exhibition in 1969 in São Paolo under the title "Images from mathematics". If you like, these were early visualisations of mathematics …

FF: And in terms of colour palettes, did you choose them?

FN: Yes, they were always my choice, totally subjective.

FF: Going back to the system that helps create the work, does that mean that, when you leave the computer to run it, you commit to any result you obtain? Or do you select some and reject others?

FN: I always select them, and reject most of them.

FF: So how does that selection process work?

FN: Well, first, you have an idea, an intention. Your program is the machine to carry out the idea. But the idea does not automatically generate only images that you will consider worth showing. So you select according to your subjective criteria. Harold Cohen's famous AARON system in its late years produced, within three minutes, something like two hundred works. Selecting from among them a much smaller number on which to do further work (by colouring) could easily take him several days. My "Matrix Multiplication" was rather successful insofar as I did not throw away many. You can see from the results that I needed quite a number of inks to do them, and the process of "painting" was rather slow. Thus, you did not want to throw away much of your precious time. By the way, these images were most likely the first in full colour that came out of a computer …

FF: These works are part of a number of variations, so, if we place all the variations of these matrix multiplications on one wall, what would we see there?

FN: What you will see is, repeated in each of the images, that in the end you get those constant columns of colours. In each of the images you see four states of the matrix (Fig. 5.2). Their sequence is (1) top left, (2) top right, (3) lower left and (4) lower right. I also did a few such images with nine states. The extra complexity adds nicely to the statement that these images make. One of those is in the Venice show. In 1968, I moved to Toronto. There, I re-implemented "Matrix Multiplication" for an interactive display. But it was only in black and white. I somehow simulated shades

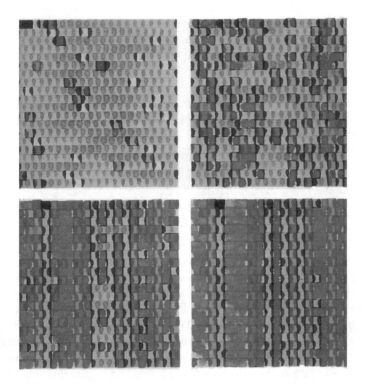

Fig. 5.2 Frieder Nake, *Matrix Multiplication series 39*, 1968. ©Frieder Nake. Courtesy of the artist

of grey. I wanted to have students sitting in front of the display and defining initial matrices. They would then run the program and observe what is happening. If they did this repeatedly, trying out different starting situations of the matrix, they should after a while observe the similarity in the processes, their limiting behaviour. They would, perhaps, create some conjecture about the character of the hidden mathematics behind the aesthetics of the events. In this way, I wanted to create visual motivations for the students to become curious about the underlying mathematics.

FF: When I see these variations I instantly think about music. So would you see them as the equivalent to that?

FN: I would use the word "variation" only in an abstract sense. There will usually be some pattern that remains largely the same, but it allows for small changes. All my experiments contained substantial amounts of randomness, often in a playful way. I came to call the use of sequences of random numbers the "simulation of intuition". Random numbers generated by the computer became the counterpart to the artist's decisions as he/she went on painting his/her canvas. I would now not say anything like this. You cannot simulate intuition. But my thinking in those long-gone early years was: if I want to do anything with a program, I must replace the artist's intuition by something that must, of course, be computable and, at the same time, appear to be unpredictable. For this, I took random numbers.

FF: So was this something you wanted to achieve in terms of computation and in terms of aesthetics?

FN: I was surprised how nice these images looked. Because of that I would say, "No, I did not *want* to achieve this, because I was *surprised*. And I loved the program". I have produced about sixty images with it. I still possess only two or three of those. All the others have been acquired by museums, or have been bought by private collectors. It was a nice success, I believe.

FF: It was. And at the same time it looks like a completely different process compared with your *hommages* to artists, like the *Hommage to Klee*, that we have here in Venice (Fig. 5.3). In that case were you trying to "force" the machine to recreate a two-dimensional image?

FN: Yes and no. I can tell you a sad anecdote behind that, and then maybe a more rational one. When I had my second exhibition, in January 1966 in Darmstadt, they showed me the August 1965 issue of the magazine *Computers and Automation*. On the cover, it displayed a computer image by A. Michael Noll, the one that simulated a painting by Piet Mondrian. I considered this quite an achievement. Later, I thought, enviously, "With that image, Noll has become rather famous". Now, I observed that, in 1965, I had often studied a booklet of rather simple drawings by Paul Klee. I liked them and I asked myself, would I be able to develop a program that could come up with something similar? I tried and the results were well received. Particularly one that, in my naming schema, became "13/9/65 Nr. 2".

Under the influence of Noll's "Computer composition with lines" (taking up Mondrian's "Composition with lines") I decided to call my image "Hommage to Paul Klee". But not only that. I now even claimed I had "simulated" Klee's drawing. This was wrong. Apparently, I wanted to catch up with Noll in simulating some artist's work. What really happened was that I had taken Paul Klee's drawings as an *inspiration* for some sort of graphic work. I much regretted my step when some journalist wrote "Nake has discovered the laws of Paul Klee, his rules. He wrote a program that he now runs, and it generates Paul Klees". What a stupid interpretation of that image! If you compare Klee's drawings from that small book with those of my program, you see only differences, but in the differences you find certain correspondences. Which, of course, is nice and hommage-like.

FF: So what was the role of the algorithm here?

FN: In this work, the algorithm simply starts by dividing the square format into separate fields. If you're thinking of those fields as rectangles, you're not wrong. But they are really "disturbed" rectangles. You see them as broken horizontal lines. The verticals remain vertical, but they are not made visible. The program "visits" each one of the grid fields to take a decision: draw a bunch of vertical lines, or of oblique lines, or do nothing. If the program decides to do nothing, it moves on into the next field. If it decides to do verticals, it must decide how many of them, and exactly where

Fig. 5.3 Frieder Nake, *Hommage à Paul Klee, 13/9/65 Nr. 2*, 1965. ©Frieder Nake. Courtesy of the artist

to put them, at random. If, thirdly, it decides for oblique lines, it must again decide how many, and from where to where? So this image is created by, most likely, several hundreds of random decisions. Building that grid, and filling it with the randomly chosen material, constitutes the *schema* of the program, the basic algorithmic idea (there are a few more aspects, though). If you take a one-by-one grid only, you get an image of only verticals or only obliques; if you take a regularly divided grid, you get all images based on a regular grid. These are subcases of the rather powerful program. If you don't like verticals or oblique lines, you put something different into the fields. You may have observed already that the "Hommage" contains another feature. If a field is made to carry verticals, and the field directly above is also to be of that kind, then you see continuation of the verticals from below. Not doing this would aesthetically be horrible. Probably, more such dependences should be explored to add more context to the construction. A second nice feature is the circles that seem to float upwards, adding a counterpoint to the otherwise straight lines. In Klee's drawings, nothing like this is contained.

FF: What amazes me is that, despite the simplicity of the rules behind it, the work actually refers directly to Klee's. How does that work?

FN: That's coincidental. You said it nicely: in spite, you said, of the simple rules that went into it, the rules were powerful enough to generate interesting visual happenings. Much complexity of a light character was created without me being in control of it. This caught up—to some extent only—with Paul Klee. It did not catch up with him completely because the lines are extremely straight and there is no hand-drawn quality. Klee's lines would also be straight, but you would feel and see the hand. The difference is the "machinic" character of my graphic.

FF: To me it also means that you really crafted the code …

FN: Well, in some way I'm proud of this image. It became one of the icons of early computer art.

FF: So why did you choose Klee in the first instance?

FN: I have no idea. Most likely I went to one of his exhibitions in Stuttgart, and I liked it. I like many of Klee's works, many I dislike, but I have at home a number of books about his work. Once I had several works of mine featuring in an exhibition at the Zentrum Paul Klee in Bern, Switzerland. That was a moment of pride for me.

FF: Once you wrote about the concept of a masterpiece, and you said that if you want to find a masterpiece in computer art you must compare algorithms. So when you look at other artists, and you compare algorithms, what would one find there?

FN: It is, of course, difficult, if not impossible, to compare two so-called masterpieces of any kind. It may be equally difficult to compare two algorithms for their merits. To be compared, these algorithms should be in the same notation as a basis for comparing them. But then, since these are explicit formal structures, we would be able to do at least something (algorithmic complexity). But now, I made this statement in the context of my conviction that there will be no masterpieces anymore. Why do I think so? Behind each and every individual computer-generated image is a program, better: an algorithm. A program is a description of a huge (really: infinite) number of possible drawings. At each and every point in time, only a few of them can be realised. It is impossible to ever see all those images that could be generated by the algorithm. So if the algorithm is the contribution, the contribution cannot be perceived. The really radical computer artist would, therefore, write the program and never let it run. To the extent that we want to apperceive the masterpiece, it can no longer exist. The masterpiece would be the infinite set which you cannot produce. The algorithm behind the "Hommage to Paul Klee" is just scratching the surface where a masterpiece could emerge.

FF: So when you look at the work of your colleagues, like Vera Molnár, Manfred Mohr, Harold Cohen, Roman Verostko, do you try to figure out what the "hidden" algorithm is? Do you search for their structure?

FN: Yes, I do, absolutely! In Vera Molnár's case, I always immediately find an algorithm. In Roman Verostko's case, it is almost always impossible because of the very fine lines he's playing with. I can only conjecture that these are "spline lines". Without asking him, I won't be able to tell. In Manfred Mohr's case, he was absolutely fantastic in his early years by often formulating in plain English enough of the algorithm that you could conjecture what was happening in the image. Later, with increasing complexity, this became more difficult. But I know his work so well that I can still often tell what is behind the surface.

FF: So again, in terms of the algorithm, what are the main differences you notice between your work and your contemporaries?

FN: There isn't much of a deep difference, I think. Mine are simplistic really, at least those until 1965. But then in 1966 I did something that is not simplistic and that nobody would be able to discover unless they knew mathematics. In 1965, the many experiments I did were always trying to take up something in straight lines, applying random numbers to them and building some kind of structure, a rather simple structure. The "Hommage to Paul Klee" stands out because the schema behind is a bit more complex. It also plays with "micro" and "macro" structures; this is again semiotics, which I did on purpose. Mohr and Cohen stand out in totally different ways, as they early on decided to follow one topic. In Mohr's case, this is the cube and the hypercube. There is hardly anyone in the world that so strictly has dealt with just one topic. Cohen's work is absolutely different. He does not start from geometry. He rather built up a system of rules that starts from something simplistic and becomes more and more complex. He is the only person who has built a program comparable in complexity to his AARON. Nobody in the world has ever done anything like this. He started by drawing closed and open forms, and then closed forms containing open forms, open forms touching, but not intersecting closed forms, a closed form inside a closed form, and so on. He did more and more of this until the closed form became a face. It contains two eyes, which are closed forms, and a nose, which is open. He discovered that if you draw an oval, and a "hook" sign into that oval, that is already enough to say it is a face. So you don't need eyes, you don't need ears, you don't need a mouth, just that "hook", that little sign, as an indication of a nose. He went as far as having almost realistic-looking (although they were never really realistic) portraits that were painted automatically. At this point in time, he decided that this was a dead end. So he returned to having only the form done by the computer, and all of the painting done by him. Harold Cohen's career is outstanding insofar as an artist has been working for thirty years and more, developing a system that nobody has any clue about. To discover his algorithmic subface is tough. In the end, Harold believed something was wrong in what he was doing. He concluded that people were more interested in the machine's operation than in his results, the images. So he turned back to where he had started from. Most amazing.

FF: I guess his objectives were different from yours …

FN: Yes, they were, absolutely. He wanted to turn the form-and-colour process into an automatic procedure on a very high level. He once said, "Deep in my heart I have always remained a colourist". His obsession was really colour. Colour, he believed in the end, you cannot control algorithmically.

FF: So what is your obsession?

FN: I'd say both colour and form. But am I obsessed? I doubt it.

FF: How would you best describe your art, both conceptually and technically?

FN: That's difficult. I think I would describe it as the visual appearance of hidden algorithms. The algorithms are the concepts; in the visual appearance, you have the perception.

FF: And do you see this as a path to be discovered by anyone?

FN: For most of my life, algorithms have been the important part in what I do. For the general public, however, the word "algorithm" became known only recently, about three years ago, with Edward Snowden's revelations. When he revealed his secrets, he used the term "algorithm", instead of "software" or "program". Since then, you can observe it appearing on TV, in newspapers, in people's everyday use. Still, it is misunderstood. People equate it with program, but algorithms are usually more complex and important than programs. They are more abstract, not depending on the formulations of a programming language. Many decades after the 1960s, our world has been transformed, through a revolution that Peter Weibel has called the "algorithmic revolution", into something we do not understand yet. Some call it the "digital epoch". We behave more and more in a way in which we must behave, because the algorithmic systems that are surrounding us and that are forcing us into certain behaviours have become ubiquitous. Algorithms are everywhere without us noticing it. And therefore I'm happy that, through some fortuitous happenstance, I came into this world of algorithmic art, because art is usually not very aggressive, it is not doing much harm to people. Other applications of algorithms are that you get shot by a drone, you lose your job because the computer has taken over, you cannot book something other than online, and so on.

FF: You just mentioned that one of your objectives was to look at colour. I noticed that this *hommage* is in black and white. In recent developments of this work you made it moving, still maintaining it in black and white. Have you thought of adding colour to that?

FN: No, colour would destroy it. I did something to it involving colour. I did two silkscreen prints of it. They were on coloured paper. One was white on dark red; the other one is green on pink. This generated a sort of psychedelic effect. But other than this, I have never thought of drawing these lines in colour because it would just be coloured, it would not make much sense to colour these lines unless you used one colour for the entire image.

FF: Is that because it focusses the attention on the structure?

FN: Yes, absolutely. And from a distance you see certain patterns standing out. On the lowest level of the drawing, the machine is acting without having a clue what it is doing. But we perceive this on various levels. We decide how we see what.

FF: Going back to your roots, would you see any link in your work that connects it with Constructivism or the constructivist tradition?

FN: That is a very interesting question. Yes, I do see links there. Why? First of all, I always liked constructivist art. Second, there are no apparent links to Constructivism in my early works, but at one point in my life something great happened. In 1966 or 1967, in London, I got to know a British constructivist artist, Anthony Hill, who, as you know, lives a double life (Hill produces and exhibits Dadaist art under the pseudonym Achill Redo). Having had an enduring fascination with mathematics, Hill and I became friends, and for a number of years even worked on a mathematical problem where we used Graph Theory to describe the black bar systems in Mondrian's neoplastic images. In my art, I can see that there is a constructive element in writing the code, the program, the algorithm: this must be strictly constructed, and you have to obey absolute rules that can be changed only by your decision in the first place.

When you think of any artists, throughout the centuries, they always have a concept. They may not always be aware of their concept, or, often, they don't like to talk about it much. But then, in the 1960s, around the time when computer art started, you also have conceptual art appearing. In 1967, Sol LeWitt publishes his "Paragraphs on Conceptual Art". One of the famous paragraphs says "The idea becomes a machine that makes the art." I did not read this when it was first published, only some time later. Then I thought, I should have written to LeWitt saying "I have read your statement, fantastic, I agree! However, I must tell you that, two years before you wrote it, I had done it already"! Algorithmic art is conceptual art brought to its end, it is radical conceptual art. Conceptual artists were cowards, they only wrote what they should do, and that the machine should do it, but they didn't build the machine!

FF: How about your future projects? I know you've been working on a number of *hommages* to artists of the past. Can you tell me more about them, and their future implications?

FN: Yes, sure. I could say, joking, that in the end I want to push myself into the world of art! How can I do that? By taking up works by artists and paying *hommage* to them. There are some famous *hommages*. Think of the meeting of Willem de Kooning with Robert Rauschenberg in 1953. Rauschenberg came to de Kooning's studio asking him to give him one of his drawings, which he, Rauschenberg, would then erase. It took a while to convince de Kooning but, in the end, Rauschenberg got what he wanted, and a new work was created: "Erased de Kooning Drawing, Robert Rauschenberg, 1953". Definitely a remarkable kind of *hommage*. In all seriousness, after having done almost inadvertently the "Hommage to Paul Klee", I am now thinking of doing a series of *hommages*. I am thinking of Gerhard Richter. I love

Gerhard Richter, because of his plethora of works. Whatever you come up with, he has done it already. He is full of ideas and has the guts not to stick to something but to do something totally new. He also used the computer, of course. I want to take one of his "strip paintings" full of very long coloured lines done digitally. I want to put them into movement, and do funny things with them. Other *hommages* would be to Roman Opałka, to Josef Albers, to Malevich, to Sol LeWitt, and more. All of them would do variations, all of them would be randomised.

FF: What draws you in particular to Richter and Malevich?

FN: When I first saw Gerhard Richter's strip paintings, I immediately loved them. I am fond of Richter's work in general but, of course, the colour field paintings and those with the thousands of coloured grid cells even more. Richter's windows in the Cologne Cathedral are another great source of inspiration to me. As for Malevich, and my *hommage* to him, I have already done three versions and had them actually exhibited. But I was not satisfied with any of them. What motivates me in his case? First, obviously, his outstanding contribution to the art of the twentieth century immediately when that century started. Like so many others, I have always considered the "Black Square" as one of the ends of painting. But now, the colour black, as paint, is the sum total of all other colours. Therefore, the one black square contains not only all the other colours. It also stands for all other paintings. This idea is the basis for my attempts to come with dynamic, ever-changing renditions, in colours breaking open and folding again.

FF: One of your works exhibited here in Venice, "Matrix Multiplication", was last exhibited in Venice on the occasion of the first exhibition of computer art at the 1970 Biennale. What are your memories of that event?

FN: Well, first of all I remember the fantastically strange title of the show, an exhibition that is a proposal of an experimental exhibition, so basically two steps of distancing yourself from what is happening there. The curators of that exhibition were rather daring: they put into that traditional and important exhibition something that in 1970—works by computers—was not really accepted. But the fact that they dared do this was a step in establishing algorithmic art as part of art history. Dietrich Mahlow, one of the curators, had done something similar just one year before in Nuremberg. And in 1968, *Tendencies 4* in Zagreb was clearly doing exactly this. Despite the great prestige of the Venice Biennale, this daring act was not really taken up by the press; there was no great reaction to this. However, looking back now almost fifty years later, I think one should recognise those events as important steps in the recognition of algorithmic art. Having my works exhibited close to Concrete and Russian constructivist art made me proud.

FF: So how do you feel about having this particular work back in Venice?

FN: I feel great about it because I'm back in Venice, this is my second time only, it was then for the 1970 Biennale, and now for this great show. Walking the streets these past days, some memories came back. Having this work back in Venice after almost fifty years feels special. The fact that I returned forty-seven years after that show does not feel as important as it feels having this show, *Algorithmic Signs*, that brings my work together with that of four other esteemed artists. It is a great experience! I know all four of them quite well. And of all the five artists in the show, my room shows the oldest works in the selection, which makes me feel proud.

FF: The title of the show is *Algorithmic Signs*. You have used this term consistently throughout your career. Can you tell us what that term means to you?

FN: I love the title you gave to the show. It is probably a bit difficult to understand; I am sure many people will not understand it. They might think, "What the hell is algorithmic signs"? To me, algorithmic signs refer in the term *signs* to those creatures, i.e. signs, that I believe determine our current culture. Our current culture is no longer determined so much by things, much more by processes, however, by processes of a semiotic kind—semiotics as the field and theory of signs. Our life has become more and more determined by sign processes. Taking this up in the term "algorithmic signs" in the title of this exhibition is to me, at least implicitly, a signal and statement about what the works on display here stand for. They stand for the time of *algorithmic processes taking command*. No longer are things the prime concern of society, but sign processes (semioses). The static images in the show stand for a principle that, in itself, is not so important. But when this principle is put into movement, it shows what characterises our time: everything is permanently changing. Nothing is stable anymore. Everything will be different the next moment. Things become relations. If I were to write a novel, in that novel this exhibition would appear as the last of its kind: computer-generated pictures on the walls of a gallery, whereas outside we would see computer-generated pictures, moving and dynamically projected onto the Venetian buildings, destroying them but only through light: they would become the carriers of the new sign processes. This is what I believe the future of these images will be.

FF: How would you explain this term to someone who does not have a mathematical background?

FN: Let's put it this way: whenever we observe some output appearing perceivably as computer output, we immediately interpret it. But we know the computer is also doing something, which we usually don't really understand. What we are witnessing there is the algorithmic sign. A sign that, at any given moment, is interpreted both by the human and by the software. It therefore has two interpretants. One of them, the computer's interpretant, however, is not the result of a genuine act of interpretation. The computer's interpretation is really a determination: determining what exactly the sign configuration stands for. The weird situation of any computer action is that, formally, it appears *as if* it were freely interpreting when in actual life it is only determining. The algorithmic sign is the reason for some people having coined the concept of "artificial intelligence". It is a phenomenon of the *as if*. It surrounds the computer in all its activities and creates a mythology and myth that is just horrible.

For it prevents people from understanding the facts. Instead, they speculate with great pleasure and zero insight. Whenever I am studying some phenomenon for its aesthetics, I try to come up with a descriptive term as soon as it becomes clear to me what is to be attributed to human perception, and what to the program's operation. We always already interpret what we see or hear or feel and we cannot do otherwise. But the computer is also doing something, which we usually don't really understand. That's, again, the reason for people's "artificial intelligence". My way of talking about the same topic is: these are sign processes, and the signs we are dealing with are signs to us and, in a limited way, to the computer as well. To both of us, they are signs, but in an unsymmetrical way. They are *algorithmic signs.*

FF: Do you see these signs as an alphabet, like a new language?

FN: Not exactly. The alphabet, or any kind of alphabet, even if you take a very broad notion of alphabet—the alphabets we know of, are always for our own human purposes. We use the alphabet as a strong way of coding, of presenting and representing some phenomena. Computers and programs do not pursue any purposes, interests, intentions. When we create a program, i.e. when we formulate a text by obeying the strict rules of the programming language, we do so in order to force the computer to do precisely what we want it to do when it is "reading" and executing the program. Unfortunately, what we call "programming language" does not share anything with a human language. It is a closed system whereas natural languages are open.

FF: Can you tell me what was your immediate reaction and feeling when you first had the opportunity to work with computers?

FN: My feeling was that I was supposed to do something that, first of all, I had no idea how to do, and second, I had a feeling that nobody else knew, either. So what was I supposed to do? To develop software that would control a computer such that it would be capable of producing and controlling a drawing machine. Whatever you wanted to draw, it would be drawn. My question became how to force a machine, that was made to compute, now to draw. I got the job, when I was about twenty-five years old, of doing something that the machine did not want to do, so I had to force it, taking it "by the hand". I had to say, "Look, you are not supposed to draw, but I will teach you". I had to make myself understand how the machine could be taught to execute the task, by thinking of drawing as a set of numerical processes, as processes that calculate and compute, and then apply this in order to compel it to create a drawing. So, in this project, I was supposed to understand what the relation between numerical processes and drawing processes was. This happened in 1963. I was lucky enough then to understand a bit of what we now all make daily use of in digital media. I did not think this way back then, but now, looking back, my feeling is that this belongs to the origins of digital media.

FF: Looking at works such as "Walk-Through-Raster" and "Matrix Multiplication" exhibited here in Venice, I notice certain visual analogies between them. Is there a particular aspect in the way they are constructed that connects them?

FN: In how the images look, you may find some analogies or even similarities. But aren't they restricted to the general appearance of images based on grids? It may be interesting, in this context, that I use two terms, i.e. "surface" and "subface" to talk about anything you do on a computer. The surface is what you see on screen, and the subface is what we do not see, which is exactly what the computer manipulates. It is interesting that surface effects may look to us a bit similar when the subfaces are totally different. I would claim that this is knowledge of a kind that emerges from the relation of the human doing something, and the computer then generating what the description requires. As with the theoretical concept of the algorithmic sign, surface and subface are tied together inseparably.

FF: So when you start to create an artwork, do you start from its "surface" or from its "subface"? In other words, between surface and subface, is there a preponderant part that takes control at the very early stages of your creative process?

FN: I would say both. The two build a dialectical unity. I'd like to say that I start from the aesthetics (and that's the external appearance). But trying to realise this as an algorithmic description requires a different kind of thinking than if you have a similar idea and take a brush or a chisel or whatever instrument you use, and try to do that by always being in control mentally and manually. I give up control in the description and therefore in that sense the algorithmic idea comes *with* the aesthetic idea.

This interview looked at how Nake has interpreted Max Bense's notion of Information Aesthetics, and how Bense's radical rationalism and semiotics have inspired his work over the years. Looking at art from a semiotic perspective, as a sign, made Nake realise how his computer programming, which was based on a repertoire of signs, could be seen similarly, through a semiotic approach.

One fascinating aspect this conversation has uncovered is the understanding of the logic process and computation behind some of Nake's most iconic works, such as *Matrix Multiplication* and *Hommage to Paul Klee,* and the commitment the artist has maintained to the mathematical procedure and organising principles in the composition of his works for over fifty years.

The following photos are of artwork on display at the exhibition, the figure number refers to the number on the map of the floor plan of exhibition which can be viewed in Chap. 7.

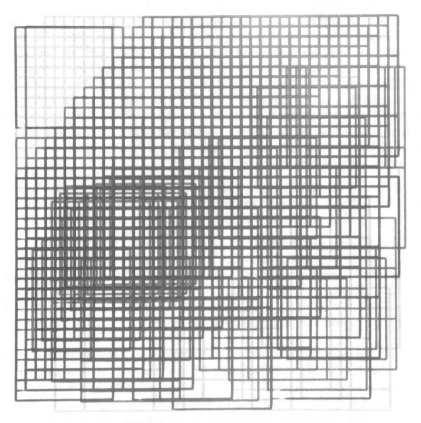

28. Frieder Nake, *Walk-through-raster Montreal version*, 1972, screenprint

29. Frieder Nake, *Random polygons*, 1964, ink on transparent paper, 10 × 10 cm each

30. Frieder Nake, *12/7/65 Bundles of straight lines*, 1965, coloured ink on paper, 82.5 × 67.2 cm

31. Frieder Nake, *Bundles of straight lines in grid*, 2015, digital print, 40 × 40 cm

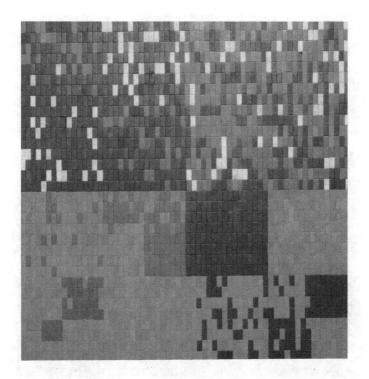

32. Frieder Nake, *Generative Aesthetics I, Experiment 6.22*, 1968/69, cardboard tiles on fiberboard, 128 × 128 cm

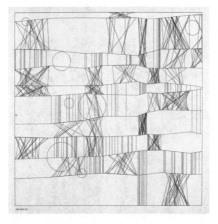

33. Frieder Nake, *13/9/65 Nr. 2 "Homage to Paul Klee"*, 1965, ink on paper, 50 × 50 cm

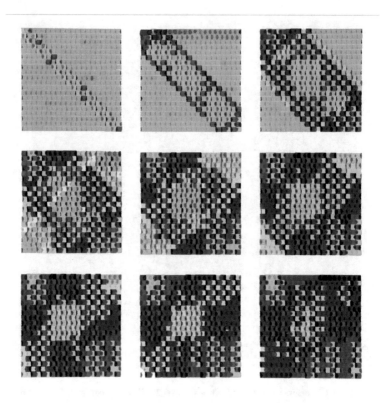

34. Frieder Nake, *Matrix multiplication series 34*, 1968, coloured ink on paper, 9 states, 40 × 40 cm

35. Frieder Nake, *Matrix multiplication series 40*, 1968, coloured ink on paper, 4 states, 40 × 40 cm

36. Frieder Nake, *Nake/ER56/264*, 1969, plotter print, 21.7 × 16.7 cm

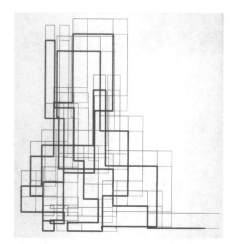

37. Frieder Nake, *25/2/65 Nr. 14 random polygon, vertical–horizontal*, 1965, coloured ink on paper, 4 colours, 42 × 55.5 cm

38. Frieder Nake, *Walk-through-raster Abteiberg version*, 2005, coloured digital print, 40 × 40 cm

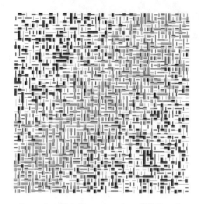

39. Frieder Nake, *Walk-through-raster Abteiberg version*, 2005, coloured digital print, 40 × 40 cm

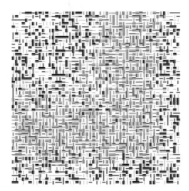

40. Frieder Nake, *Walk-through-raster Abteiberg version*, 2005, coloured digital print, 40 × 40 cm

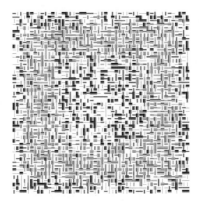

41. Frieder Nake, *Walk-through-raster Abteiberg version*, 2005, coloured digital print, 40 × 40 cm

References

Bense, Max (1965). "Projekte generativer ästhetik". Available online at www.computerkunst.org/ Bense_Manifest.pdf. [Accessed 26 August 2018].

Nake, Frieder (1971). "There Should Be No Computer Art", *PAGE: Computer Arts Society Bulletin* 18 (October), 18–19. Available online at http://www.bbk.ac.uk/hosted/cache/archive/PAGE/PAG E18.pdf. [Accessed 25 August 2018].

Nake, Frieder (2010). "Paragraphs on Computer Art, Past and Present", CAT 2010 conference, British Computer Society, 3 February 2010. Available online at http://dada.compart-bremen.de/ item/publication/397. [Accessed 18 June 2018].

Chapter 6
Interview with Roman Verostko

Interviews Recorded in Sheffield, 19 November 2012, and London, 8 February 2017

Born in the USA in 1929, Roman Verostko is best known for his richly coloured algorithmic pen and brush drawings. His approach to art grew from the theory and practice of early-twentieth-century artists like Piet Mondrian, Wassily Kandinsky and Kazimir Malevich. As an artist, Verostko has been influenced by what Henri Focillon described as "the life of forms" in art, particularly his notion of how art forms change over time.

Although schooled primarily as a painter, he experimented with other media and, in the late 1960s, created a series of electronically synchronised audio-visual programs presented as the "Psalms in Sound & Image". As a Bush fellow at MIT in 1970, the year in which Verostko came to the realisation that, through computer programming and coded procedures, one could generate and explore an immense world of visual forms, he set out to "humanise our experience of emerging technologies". Also in 1970 he took a course in Fortran at the Control Data Institute in Minneapolis, where he learned how to write elementary drawing instructions with algorithms. With these instructions he could mimic procedures and drawing techniques he had previously been using in his art.

It was the advent of the personal computer a decade later that allowed Verostko to fully commit himself to the development of new art forms using the power of algorithmic recursive drawing as the original source for his creative practice. By 1982, with his own studio PC, he had exhibited his first fully algorist work, "The Magic Hand of Chance".

From this experience he developed his own master drawing program to guide both ink pens and brushes with multipen drawing machines. It is a practice that he has developed and refined over the years, and that he still uses to generate art. The plotter, coupled to a PC and guided with his own original software, chooses from an array of pens loaded with pigmented inks and draws each individual line. Works such as "Diamond Lake Apocalypse" (1991) and the "Cyberflowers" series (2000–) require thousands of lines and sometimes brush strokes generated by the machine's drawing arm. In some cases, works are enhanced with the use of gold or silver leaf applied by hand.

© Springer Nature Switzerland AG 2022
F. Franco, *The Algorithmic Dimension*, Springer Series on Cultural Computing,
https://doi.org/10.1007/978-3-319-61167-9_6

In 2008 he merged past and present by transforming his 1970s drawings into a stunning array of digital images for an Upsidedown Book and Mural for the Fred Rogers Center, Latrobe, PA, USA. In 2010 his show *Algorithmic Poetry* in Berlin celebrated nature via visual forms generated with brushes and ink pens driven with his algorithms.

Verostko has been the recipient of several awards, including the 2009 SIGGRAPH Distinguished Artist Award for Lifetime Achievement; *Artec'95*, Recommendatory Prize, Nagoya, Japan; Golden Plotter Award, Germany, 1994; Professor Emeritus, MCAD, 1994; Prix Ars Electronica, Honorable Mention, 1993; Director, ISEA 1993; Bush Fellow, Center for Advanced Visual Studies, MIT, 1970; and Outstanding Educators of America, 1971 and 1974.

Francesca Franco: The first thing that struck me about your work is the way it is created using a pen plotter. It reminds me of the miniatures of old medieval manuscripts. My first question is, is there a connection between the two elements?

Roman Verostko: Yes. During my monastic years I had come to appreciate medieval manuscript illumination and that experience had an immense influence on my later work with the pen plotter. About twenty years later, in my Minneapolis studio, I acquired my first pen plotter, a Houston Instruments DM P52 with fourteen pen stalls—a marvellous drawing machine! Soon my master's program, *Hodos*, was generating code for drawing some of my art-form ideas. By the late 1980s I had acquired several plotters and began to view my plotters as my *electronic scriptors*. These plotters became my twentieth-century electronic *scriptorium*. I gave my plotters names like Brunelleschi, Alberti and Giotto. Besides writing code for drawing my art-form ideas, I had developed some glyphic text sequences that are present in some of my earliest routines for "The Magic Hand of Chance". My first scripts for the pen plotter are found in my *Hodos Correspondence*. These scripts were drawn on standard bond paper sized for writing letters. The texts were, to my mind, at that time, "glyphs" that did not have any meaning, but they did simulate language. The frequency of character appearance mimicked frequencies found in the English language. My "Diamond Lake Apocalypse" series was the first to mimic medieval manuscript illumination. Each work in the series had one side of the work with glyphic texts and the other side with a drawing meant to be an illumination. I conceived of this work as an opened manuscript showing the left and right pages. Other scripts to follow were my *Illuminated Universal Turing Machines*, *Sixty-four DNA Codons* and my *Pearl Park Scriptures*.

FF: In some of your articles you use the term "algorist". Can you tell me more about this term?

RV: Yes, I identify myself as an algorist but I continue to view my work as "generative art". In the late 1980s, as commercial software became available for artists, historians had no term to distinguish those artists who wrote their own code from those who used commercial software. Artists like Harold Cohen, Herbert Franke, Manfred Mohr and many more had been creating art with their own code for over twenty years and their work was called "computer art". They were the pioneers of a radically new approach to creating art. With control of their software they were coding for their own art ideas. In the late 1980s I was impressed with some of the algorithmic drawings by Jean-Pierre Hébert, who lived in Santa Barbara, north of Los Angeles. We became friends, and I would often visit with him and his family on my California trips. We shared concerns about paper, pens, inks and code. So, we ended up participating in SIGGRAPH, ISEA and regional events. Following one of these conferences, where Peter Beyles chaired a panel on "Algorithms and the Artist", the identity subject arose. We needed an identity for those who wrote their own software. There was no term commonly used at that time. Terms like "algorithmic artist" and "algorithmicist" didn't work well. Hébert, with his French background, suggested that we use the term "algorist", the term for anyone who wrote algorithms. So, artists who write their own algorithms are "algorists". We began using the term to identify artists who had been writing algorithms for creating their art since the 1960s and those who were currently active as "algorists". This includes the new generation of artists like Casey Reas, who has introduced processing language that has spawned a new generation of algorists.

FF: And where does the term "epigenetic" come from?

RV: "Epigenetic" was a term that I used for my art process in my paper at the First International Symposium on Electronic Art in Utrecht in 1988, *Epigenetic Art: Software as Genotype* (Utrecht, 1988 ISEA). This paper identifies the biological analogues for generative art. There are three terms to understand: *genotype, epigenesis* and *phenotype*. In biological terms a "seed" that contains all the necessary code for growing a plant is called a "genotype". The process of growing the plant is called "epigenesis". This process requires soil, water nutrients and carbon dioxide. The mature plant is called a "phenotype". By analogy, my master code for generating a drawing may be viewed as a "genotype". Like the seed, it has all the detailed instruction necessary for generating my drawing. The process of generating the drawing requires a computer, a pen plotter, paper, ink and ink pens. That process of executing the code, with paper, pen and ink, may be likened to growing the plant; it "grows" the drawing in a manner likened to biological "epigenesis". The finished pen and ink drawing may be likened to the "phenotype", the mature plant. While the analogy holds up well, it is not easily understood, so I prefer using the term Generative Art for my art. The "epigenesis" analogy is a bit difficult to explain, yet it helps us understand better the many analogies between biological processes and emerging intelligent robotics. It is the most accurate term for the process underlying my work. I continue to be very deeply interested in the "epigenetic" process. I did revisit "Epigenetic Art" with an exhibition and a paper for the 2003 *Ars Electronica* symposium on *Code: The Language of Our Time* and a decade earlier for their 1993 *Genetic Art—Artificial Life* symposium. (See the notes at the end of this chapter for access to those papers.)

Fig. 6.1 Roman Verostko, *Three Story Drawing Machine*, 2011. ©Roman Verostko. Image courtesy of the artist

FF: Do you see your code as a score, like a musical score?

RV: I like to point to a musical score as an algorithm or a code for a musical idea. This helped me understand code better, and it has helped me explain code for my students and others. An algorithm for drawing a visual form may be likened to a score for playing music. Both are codes for an art form. I recall one occasion, many years ago, when the St Paul Chamber Orchestra played Beethoven's Ninth. At the end of the symphony the entire audience stood up and applauded, a very enthusiastic applause with extended curtain calls. And I thought to myself, at that moment, "my goodness, that score is the code for a musical idea that was in Beethoven's mind over 150 years ago". He couldn't hear well but he probably heard the music in what I would call his *"mind-ear"*, pretty much like I visualise a form-generating idea in my "mind-eye". Consequently, inasmuch as musicians interpret his code, the score, in the way Beethoven intended, we have his music present for us now. His musical concept for the Ninth, embedded in his score, may be viewed as an algorithm. In my paper on "Epigenetic Art: Software as Genotype" I would view his score as a "genotype". The score embodies all the information necessary for playing the music. That's pretty much like one of my master algorithms for a work of art.

FF: In Venice, we were honoured to see on video (Fig. 6.1) how your drawing machine works. Do you want to tell us a bit more about how the machine works?

RV: The eight-hour video shown in Venice documents a pen plotter's drawing arm as it draws my "Green Cloud" Cyberflower from the very first stroke to the end of the process that includes a calligraphic text. This video was created for projection on the three-storey north wall of the Minneapolis College of Art and Design as a feature of

Fig. 6.2 Roman Verostko,
The Canticle of the Sun,
1995. ©Roman Verostko.
Image courtesy of the artist

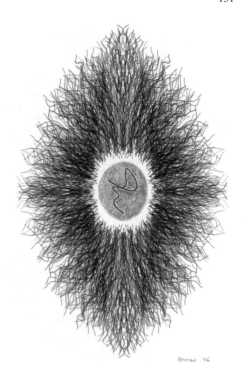

Northern Spark's 2011 "White Night" in Minneapolis. A "White Night", beginning at sunset, is an all-night celebration of the arts. We taped the eight-hour video for this work in my studio. I kept the plotter alive, non-stop, for over eight hours of drawing time. Earlier I had sampled six to eight versions until I achieved the drawing time to fit an exact window of time from sunset on 4 June to sunrise on 5 June 2011. For me it was a technical thing to get precisely correct down to the minute. I built an extra tall inkwell for the pen so I wouldn't have to change pens in that eight-hour period. We used one of my Hi-Plot 8000 plotters named "Alberti". By 1990 I had at least three active pen plotters in my studio that I viewed as my electronic *scriptorium*.

FF: The work shown in the video is called "Cyberflower". Do you want to tell us more about this specific work?

RV: Yes, my first Cyberflowers date from around 1988. They were a series of drawings generated with my "radiant" routine that yielded a series of drawings in an elliptical format. These were mounted in gold-leafed oval frames for a regional 1989 exhibition. An art historian colleague, upon seeing the drawings, exclaimed with some excitement "These drawings are Cyberflowers!" That "radiant routine" evolved into my celebrations of the sun as in "The Canticle of the Sun" (1995) (Fig. 6.2).

Years later, with a recursive routine playing with a single set of initial coordinates, my code generated a form that I found satisfying and surprisingly like the historic moment when my colleague declared "Cyberflowers"! These Cyberflowers were

Fig. 6.3 Roman Verostko, *The Flowers of Learning (Madame Curie)*, 2006. ©Roman Verostko. Image courtesy of the artist

born in cyberspace and I felt they were the bloom of my coded procedures. Some of the Cyberflowers, as in "The Flowers of Learning" (Fig. 6.3) have texts on the bottom that are excerpts of wisdom from different cultures.

The "Flowers of Learning" I think represent for me that new code, that new liberation, that I'm now free without any dogma, without anything on my shoulders, to read whatever I want and understand whatever I am able to understand, and what I don't understand, that's OK, too. In other words I'm not bound anymore, I am free. Seven of them are part of a large permanent installation that I created for the Spalding University Academic Center in Louisville, Kentucky. Dedicated to educators, those seven Cyberflowers, mounted in a 25-ft frame, are conceived as a *"hortus conclusus"*, an enclosed garden. In medieval art and architecture an enclosed garden symbolised the "heavenly place". For me the educational institution is an enclosed garden, the place where knowledge liberates us. My Cyberflowers celebrate educators and education as a garden of delights with enlightenment and freedom.

FF: The work that we have just seen, drawing from sunrise to sunset, looks pretty much like a spiritual experience, a spiritual event. How is your work influenced by your experience as a monk?

RV: Well, I think that every moment of my life, the total complex of my life experience, transcends my understanding. Any moment, at any time, may be the occasion for an experience that one might call "spiritual". The "Flowers of Learning", and the Cyberflowers in general, gave me a greater appreciation for the awesome power of recursive functions. When I watched the unfolding of some of my first Cyberflower forms I was amazed. The power of a few lines of recursive code bringing life to a form is awesome. Is that a spiritual experience? For me those elevated moments we experience in music and the visual arts transcend rational understanding. From that perspective you might speak of those moments as a spiritual experience. Perhaps the big thing for me, following my monastic life, was the realisation that I don't need to believe in anything that is not believable to myself. Better you have an unanswered question than embracing something unbelievable to yourself. And that's pretty much what I do in my artwork. I probe the mysterious nature of our "being here".

FF: Like all those who know your life story, I'm fascinated by how you got into art through a very unique path that crossed so many different avenues and life experiences. Can you tell me more about the most significant steps that led you to choose art in your life?

RV: Circumstances, at each stage of my life, kept the practice of art in my life. In truth, I always did like drawing from the time I entered grade school. But I also loved just about everything I studied. In 1947, my senior-year paper for Physics examined the underlying physics of the atomic bomb. I had hoped to go to college and become a physicist, but without money and guidance I was pretty much on my own. I also wanted to be an illustrator like Norman Rockwell. I loved his illustrations for the Saturday Evening Post in the 1930s and 1940s. His work was really something. Circumstances unfolded in a way that made it possible for me to go to the Art Institute of Pittsburgh. I found an evening job as a grill chef that helped pay my tuition. I learnt how to do portraits from Vincent Nesbert (b. 1898), who emigrated to the USA in 1914 and joined the Art Institute of Pittsburgh in 1928. He was a fantastic classical painter from Poland, he taught me a lot about portraiture; and I studied with Harry L. Hickman, who was a landscape artist, and he would take us on his river boat down the river, so I learnt how to do watercolours, landscapes, but also typography, so all these were skills I learnt then. I graduated in 1949 when we were getting deeply involved with the Korean War. I also had memories of my brother being killed in Germany in 1945, and the other terrible parts of World War 2. I was of draft age and I was looking for something more. I began exploring how I might manage to go on to graduate school, but I was attracted to monastic life. I had read Thomas Merton's *Seven Storey Mountain* (1948) and was drawn to monastic life. In 1950, on my twenty-first birthday, I made the decision that I would join the monastery. I made an oil painting on canvas in the process, before entering my Novitiate year (1952–53), and I don't think I will ever forget this. It's called "Deciding" (*c.* 1951). I think all of us at that time had been affected by the horrific experiences of World War 2, and then all the repercussions of that. Many young men at that time went into monasteries; there was a turn towards religion, and I followed that path.

FF: So, how did that life work out for you as an artist?

RV: That was uncertain for me at first. I entered with the pathway towards the priest-hood. During those first eight years I studied classical languages, philosophy and theology and was eventually ordained as a priest. But there was also a studio available for me. During free time I engaged in studio projects throughout my monastic years. We ran a major seminary and a college, so many of us were sent for higher education to different universities. So, I was sent to learn all I could about art and was able to continue my studio practice along with academic studies in New York and Paris.

The monastery had an arrangement with St Michael's Parish located on West 34th Street between 9 and 10th Avenue. In exchange for residence and a studio space while pursuing advanced studies, I provided some priest services. I heard confessions on Saturdays, celebrated one of the Sunday Masses and the daily Mass for the Sisters who ran an Academy on 33rd Street. During the week I was free to do all my studies and go wherever I wanted to study. So, I went to Pratt Institute for a master's degree. I then followed graduate courses at the New York Institute of Fine Arts and Columbia University. There was a whole world that I've lived in besides the art world. I understood what was happening in Manhattan, because I lived in Mid-town just as they finished writing the musical "West Side Story". The residence was located on the West side, close to the Hudson River, and in those days there were about seventy ports along the Hudson River, and daily many ships came and left. That neighbourhood was Irish Catholic in its time, but when I arrived the change was on and it was becoming populated by people from Cuba, Mexicans were coming, we had a Spanish-speaking community which was the basis for "West Side Story", but I understood "West Side Story" right from the heart, because I lived in a parish that itself had to go through that division, so we had priests that were Irish, others that were fluent in Spanish … So I learnt a lot about the social conditions of this area now known as Hell's Kitchen, and I painted a number of canvases that were intended as a social commentary on the ethnic transformations of that area at that time. At the same time, I learned a lot about the art world in Manhattan. This was the period of Abstract Expressionism when I could go down to The Village for those Friday nights when the artists got together and discussed the issues. It was a kind of a strange mix because I wore a Roman collar and I would even get invited to loft parties and private openings. I painted canvases experimenting with geometric painting as well as others intended as social commentary on ethnic transformations of that area. Thus, my geometric work "Morning Sunshine on West 34th Street"

(Fig. 6.4), "Monk on West 34th Street" and an "Irish Housekeeper" standing in front of the church entrance where the St Michael Church was identified as "San Miguel".

In the summer of 1962 I was invited to a Harper's Bazaar party in an Upper East Side apartment where I met Andy Warhol and John Chamberlain. What surprised me when I walked in on the ground floor was a receptionist with papers to sign, where I was asked to sign a document in case they used one of my pictures. I was sure that it would be respectable so I signed off, and here you have a picture of me in Harper's Bazaar, chatting with John Chamberlain, next to Andy Warhol. I was escorted to the apartment and was first introduced to Andy Warhol; we talked a while. Warhol and I were born in the same year and he would have been at Carnegie Mellon in Pittsburgh about the same time that I had been at the Art Institute of Pittsburgh. The Harper's Bazaar party was meant to be who's who in Manhattan. I remember they referred to me as "Father Roman, the Geometric artist priest", because in my studio they had seen some geometric artwork as I was influenced by constructivists at that time.

I also got to know Allan Kaprow, who wanted me to do a Eucharistic service in a hotdog stand as pop art, so we would have a pop art holy mass! I was interested in that as an artistic proposition, but I didn't have the freedom in my personhood and didn't want to be offensive to my order, but on the other hand maybe Kaprow had a point.

At that time, I developed a close friendship with Stephen Joy, a curator at Martha Jackson Gallery, which was an important gallery in those days. We became friends, and eventually he became my agent. He had helped curate shows at Martha Jackson that included works such as Allan Kaprow's "Yard" in 1961. Simultaneously, I had the opportunity to work with Fritz Eichenberg and Andy Stasik at Pratt Institute's new Graphic Art Centre in Manhattan, on 6th Avenue close to The Village. There I learned of the post-World War 2 revival of printmaking and the work of Stanley William Hayter in Paris, who had influenced the print revival in New York.

FF: So, when was the moment you decided to start using formal procedure to produce new work?

RV: It began through my friend and art critic, Stephen Joy. On my occasional New York visits in 1967 and 1968 he encouraged me to pay attention to the growing interest in Electronics Art and Technology, E.A.T. Around that time, I acquired an electronic synchroniser, projectors, carousels, a camera stand and a Wollensak tape recorder. I began working with electronically synchronised audio-visuals and presented my first synchronised program for a spiritual retreat in the fall of 1966. This experimental work included a soundtrack by Lucia Dlugoszewski and slides composed from my own drawings and photos. The music was recorded on one soundtrack and the other was programmed with an electronic synchroniser to trigger the slides. Projection from floor to ceiling and amplified speakers provided a memorable audio-visual experience. That was my first programming experience. During that period I had already come to realise that I would leave my religious life. It is interesting that in 1967–68, just before I left religious life, I went to MIT for the dedication of the newly established Centre for Advanced Visual Studies (CAVS) founded by György Kepes and conceived as a fellowship programme for artists. I was very interested in his work and his thinking, and at the time I was taking an interest in the humanisation of emerging technologies, so when I got the grant from the Bush Foundation I got the opportunity to do some further investigations and studies in that field. What happened is I went to MIT, lived in Boston, and learnt quite a bit.

FF: So where did your plans take you then?

RV: I left the monastery in May of 1968 and found a position on the humanities faculty at the Minneapolis College of Art and Design, where I taught world art history. Minnesota, surprisingly, was one of the centres for computing in the USA at that time. It was the home of Control Data, Honeywell and Cray Research, with UNIVAC located in St Paul, its Twin City. The founder of the first firm to manufacture supercomputers, Seymour Roger Cray, was from the University of Minnesota, and was the cofounder, with William Norris, of Control Data Corporation, one of the major computer companies in the USA in the 1960s. So I was pretty soon introduced, as someone interested in electronic arts and technology, to the world of emerging electronic technologies, and in the college we were interested in getting people on the board who were interested in joining art and technology. So it was natural for me to explore these paths. Also, because the husband of one of our board members,

Dr Piero Morawetz, was starting up one of the many corporations (Tetra Corporation Minneapolis), this is where I learnt a lot, too. In 1969 he invited me to be his
"Humanities Consultant" for the Tetra Corporation. I was invited, in my free time,
to hang around the development labs where I could learn something about circuit
boards and how they were designed and made. He wanted Tetra to emerge with
more than just technical interests; he wanted a connection to the arts, understanding
that I was interested in computer art. This experience led me to follow a course in
programming at the Control Data Institute in the Spring of 1970. So that was my first
experience in 1968–70. Then, on top of that, I wanted a direction for myself. I had
left monastic life, and I realised there was the Bush Foundation and I could apply
for a grant there. I applied and I got it, so in 1970 I became Visiting Scholar as Bush
Leadership Fellow at the Center For Advanced Visual Studies, MIT.

Within a decade I had my first PC, with my first showing of "The Magic Hand of
Chance" in 1982. I committed my studio to electronic art, and by 1987 I had several
plotters in my Pathway Studio that I came to view as my electronic *scriptorium*.

FF: I'd like to go through some of your most accomplished algorithmic works and
look at the technical aspects that characterise the way they were initially planned and
then executed.

RV: Let me explain one thing up front about the term "random" and computers.
Computers are determined systems that cannot make a random choice. The
computer's operating system includes a "pseudo-randomiser" that simulates random
behaviour. For both artistic and scientific purposes this pseudo-randomiser serves
us well both in the sciences and in the arts. While the computer's randomiser is a
pseudo-randomiser we commonly refer to it as a *randomiser.*

When I made this "Gaia" from the V&A collection (Figs. 6.5 and 6.6), I had
been working on random colour selection since the early 1980s with my "Magic
Hand of Chance". With my pen plotting code I was reaching very hard to get to
that point where the colour choices made by the code, in conjunction with other
random choices, would be satisfying to myself. Now, how could I achieve that? In
the end there was no absolute formula, but the challenge for me was something like
this: to get my master code set with parameters of "not more than" and "not less
than" a given ink pen from a palette of ink pens. The code then "throws dice" within
pre-set limits for choosing a pen. In a similar way the number of strokes for the
chosen pen and the starting position, angle and scale for each stroke were also set.
The challenge is to get a default setting that yields a distribution that is satisfying
for myself. This Gaia would be one of the examples where I felt that I had begun to
succeed. A few years later, when I achieved my "Canticle of the Sun" series I did so
with considerable confidence. The "Canticle of the Sun" shown in Venice (Fig. 6.2)
is an excellent example where the choice of ink pens and the pen stroke distributions
were essentially random decisions. I learned this from Stephen Orey, who introduced
me to probability theory. He was the one who led to me to read George Boole's work.

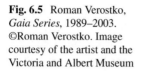

Fig. 6.5 Roman Verostko, *Gaia Series*, 1989–2003. ©Roman Verostko. Image courtesy of the artist and the Victoria and Albert Museum

FF: In terms of colour choices, were all these colours your choice in the code or is there some level of randomness applied to this choice?

RV: I choose the colours for my palette of pens and I mix the colours. They are lightfast acrylic inks that I usually mix for about a 50% transparency. Each pen has a number. I also choose the paper, select the pen sizes, and set the plotter drawing speed. My code makes the pen choices and those choices are effectively colour choices. If I am generating a series in a family of forms I use the same palette of ink pens for every work in the series. My colour mixes have various degrees of transparency, shade and hue, so we get glazing when they overlap. The pen stroke overlaps are important factors. For this work, there is, I believe, a palette of five inks: one with a blue base, one yellow, one red, and so on; the code uses the randomiser in the process of pen decisions. However, it works with filters that have conditions of acceptability. Conditions may want a number or a factor aspect of "not more than" and "not less than" such and such a number for a pen. And there may be other subloop conditions.

Fig. 6.6 Roman Verostko, *Gaia Series* (detail), 1989–2003. ©Roman Verostko. Image courtesy of the artist and the Victoria and Albert Museum

The randomiser works until it gets a number that passes through the filters. My master's program grew for over fifteen to twenty years, becoming a code embedded with my preferences and interests as an artist. Most variable factors, in my program, are selected via the randomiser and filters with parameters of "not more than" and "not less than". There are settings in my master's program for many factors for each pen stroke: colour, angle for springing the stroke, coordinates initiating the stroke, the scale via radius from one point to the next control point in the curve, etc. There are about seventy to eighty factors that are set every time my program runs—all variables have defaults. So, when I write a data file for a specific set of parameters and options, it over-rides default settings, but many defaults are rarely changed. The data file contains essential parameters for the form, colour options, size and other details necessary for the drawing.

FF: So, does that mean that once you have set the code you are committed to any result you get?

RV: Yes, provided I am satisfied with the first one. Chances are that everyone to follow with a new seed will be acceptable. In the case of "Twenty-Six Visions of Hildegarde" (Fig. 6.7), I set one master parent code, and all twenty-six visions followed, using the same parent code. The differences follow from the new "seed", the number that initiates the randomiser. With a new seed, the randomiser will generate a new number sequence. The palette remains the same, and all parameter limits such as "not more

Fig. 6.7 Roman Verostko, *Twenty-Six Visions of Hildegarde*, 2004. ©Roman Verostko. Image courtesy of the artist

than" and "not less than" remain the same. But, the random choice will vary for every variable factor in the data file. For the twenty-six visions the sequence yields twenty-six variations in a family of familial forms because all are generated from the same parent code.

FF: Does that mean that you are always happy with the result?

RV: No, that is the issue. Can you get to the point where you are happy with every drawing? That was Harold Cohen's problem, my problem, and a problem for everyone who works with generative art. Now, to understand this, you might think of Hans Arp, who took paper, and dropped it to fall wherever it would. Well, maybe it went here, maybe it went there. He could drop paper from a second-storey window and let it fall wherever it might. On the other hand, he might lay a stretched canvas on the floor and accept only those pieces he drops that fall within the bounds of the canvas. Those who work with chance are always bound to set parameters. So usually you set parameters that can be loose or tight, depending on preferences for a specific family of form.

FF: I understand that the Chinese brush tradition had a direct influence on the software that you created. So, what are the main lessons you have learnt from that that you find particularly inspiring?

RV: What I have learned isn't entirely new because I had already practised brush in my Abstract Expressionist period in New York and I was aware that there was an oriental influence in abstract expressionism. But, in 1985, after Chinese master calligrapher Wang Dongling followed my course in China and demonstrated his work for me, everything changed. I brought Chinese brushes back to my studio. The other factor was the code I wrote in 1986 for a sequence of strokes that looked somewhat like a language. This would lead me to appreciate the software control I could have of the stroke. Soon I developed the routines for my first brush strokes. Since then my pen and brush strokes took on something of the character of oriental calligraphy. This was especially strong in my four works for the *Artec'95* show in Nagoya, Japan. My Algorithmic Poetry works are excellent examples as well as the scripting for "Floating Cloud".

FF: From a technical point of view, when you use the brush and the pen plotter in your algorithmic drawings, I notice the brush strokes and drawing lines are immaculate, so, for instance in this "Frog Jump" (Fig. 6.8), how could you technically achieve these perfect brush strokes, without dripping, etc.?

RV: I will explain that. Let me note first that there are seventeen brush strokes presented as a sort of visual *haiku*. The seventeen large strokes are repeated in the vertical column of seventeen strokes. The large black brush stroke was done last, but the code repeats this stroke as the first one in the column of seventeen small brush strokes.

How did I do those seventeen large strokes without dripping? Some of my brush strokes do have dripping and sometimes I lose a work. For the most part I am careful about how I load the brush and it is never allowed to be in the brush holder except when brushing. I built a coded routine that sets the plotter to a brush mode, and my monitor reminds me that "brush mode is on". With "brush mode on" my code moves the plotter drawing arm to a position for the stroke; then it says, "give me the brush"; I dip the brush in the ink and place it in the plotter's drawing arm and then I hit a key

Fig. 6.8 Roman Verostko, *Frog Jump*, 2010. ©Roman Verostko. Image courtesy of the artist

and it executes the stroke, then it stops, lifts the brush and says, "remove the brush". I remove the brush. I went through this routine for each of the seventeen strokes. For the vertical calligraphic strokes, I used a small self-inking brush that works like an ink pen, so the brush can move from one stroke to the next without stopping.

For the "Frog Jump" brush strokes I wanted to achieve some of the character of my abstract expressionist work, and I think these two last works I just described are among my most important and achieved works.

FF: So, of all your production, which are the works you are most proud of?

RV: I'm very proud of many. From my pre-monastic work I would choose "One Way" from my moralising scratchboard drawings that date from 1949. From my monastic period I would choose one of my 1960s "New City" paintings and the Ceramic Mural in the St Vincent College Library in Latrobe, PA, USA. Of my pre-algorist work I would single out my drawings for my "Upsidedown Mural" at the Fred Rogers Early Childhood Learning Centre in Latrobe, PA, USA. The original drawings were created from 1968 to 1975 in Minneapolis. They were adapted for the panels for the two-storey mural and installed in 2008.

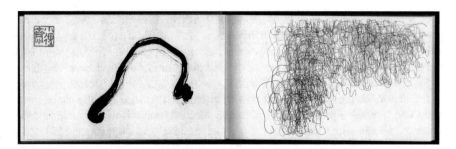

Fig. 6.9 Roman Verostko, *Derivation of the laws of the symbols of logic from the laws of the operations of the human mind: an excerpt from George Boole's Investigation of the Laws of Thought*, 1991. ©Roman Verostko. Image courtesy of the artist and the Anne and Michael Spalter Digital Art Collection

As for my algorithmic works, I would choose three projects. (1) From 1989–1990, my Illustrated limited edition of Chap. 3 from George Boole's *Investigation of the Laws of Thought* (Fig. 6.9). (2) My 1997 installation of *Epigenesis: The Growth of Form*, a 40-ft installation of eleven algorithmic drawings at the University of St Thomas' Science and Engineering Center, in St Paul Minnesota would be one of the greatest of my lifetime achievements. (3) The *Flowers of Learning* permanent installation of seven Cyberflowers as an enclosed garden mounted in a 25-ft frame, at Spalding University in Louisville, Kentucky. This project achieved seven painterly algorithmic drawings in a family of Cyberflower forms that speak eloquently of the texts they illuminate.

FF: And in terms of programming, which works are you most proud of?

RV: I would identify my *Magic Hand of Chance* and *Hodos* as my two most important programs. *The Magic Hand of Chance*, one of the first generative art programs ever written for an IBM PC, pointed to the emerging power of the PC as a platform for artists.

Hodos, my master's program for drawing with my pen plotter, is my most important program as an algorist. This program integrates routines that draw on a common set of variables for any number of subroutines. The program allows me to draw on one or several routines for a given project or series of works. Or I can add a new routine tomorrow. *Hodos*, which is now in its sixth version, has evolved over a period of about thirty years. This program is my attempt to create an expert system capable of generating artworks that embody my art ideas. There is a user interface. Anyone who learns the interface would be able to generate my art forms.

FF: So, is there a relationship between order and randomness in your work?

RV: Yes, the junction of randomness and order has permeated most my work since the 1960s. I use plain geometry with a Cartesian grid in structuring my procedures. I don't approach my work as a mathematician. I create my algorithms as an artist with certain experienced ideas about how to create my art. Ordinarily I think of an algorithm as a procedure for doing something. So, I might want code to mimic something about how I proceeded in my work when I practised a form of automatism. When I first began I wanted to achieve an automatism generated by the nature of the computer itself. That led me to study George Boole's *Investigation of the Laws of Thought* and Alan Turing's work with *Computable Numbers*. I became interested in the history of the computer and how it emerged. It seemed like the easiest way would be to write a procedure for pixels to succeed each other in a random walk. One could begin with a simple procedure such as this: "move up one, and left one", or, with a randomiser, you might write a code that says "move up any number from one to ten", or "move left any number from one to ten", or one could have a sequence of procedures that would be a "loop" for generating a sequence of visual events in pixels that would be indeed a random walk. But once you provide those parameters, you are introducing control. As I proceeded to evolve the *Magic Hand of Chance* and my code for *Hodos*, it turned out that every line or pen stroke, in one way or another, involved the conjunction of both random behaviour and some form of control.

FF: So, what would you say are the foundations of your compositions?

RV: I think the most important part of my career emerged from a spiritual side, something that you get both in western spirituality and in oriental thought. I found conflict between emotional passionate experiences and my thoughtful rational experiences in life. How do we resolve this conflict of opposites? I can point to a series of paintings that I made called the "New City" that drew on human experience where you have passion, spontaneity and vigorous life experiences driving you one way while your rational, reasonable self draws you another way. I wrestled with the resolution of these opposites by placing expressive and passionate brush and drawing strokes in the same picture field with highly controlled harmonic rectangular forms. These paintings wrestled with visual oppositions. How could I bring them to a peaceful visual resolution? This involves every aspect of life, the masculine and the feminine, day and night, hard and soft, light and dark, sweet and sour. It's all those things, and my "New City" paintings of the 1960s played with this resolution of opposites. Even in works such as "The Magic Hand of Chance", I was constantly setting up a random set of events within certain controlling parameters and then sometimes I introduce a very rigid discipline, and at the same time I always tried to marry apparent visual contradictions. Confrontation of the resolution of opposites lies at the core of most of my life and my work. In my algorithmic art practically, every pen stroke engages "throws of the dice" within controlling parameters; one could view my entire experience as a conjunction of "chance and control"; it is present throughout both my life and my art.

Verostko's introduction to the art world and the way it formed and developed have followed a unique path. This conversation has uncovered details about Verostko's early education, how his priesthood years have informed his art, his "New York years", and the steps that lead Verostko to start learning programming formal procedures and electronically synchronised audio-visuals in his art practice. It also looked at the technical aspects and foundations of some of his more accomplished algorithmic works, such as the Gaia Series and Twenty-Six Visions of Hildegarde.

The following photos are of artwork on display at the exhibition, the figure number refers to the number on the map of the floor plan of exhibition which can be viewed in Chap. 7.

43. Roman Verostko, *Untitled*, 1963, brush, watercolour and crayon, 73 × 93 cm

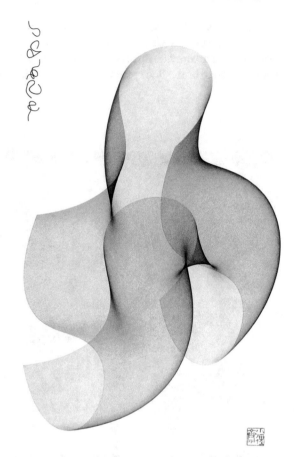

44. Roman Verostko, *Morning Song*, 2010, plotter drawing, pen and brush on paper, 76 × 56 cm

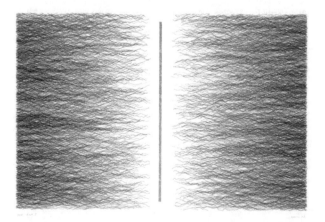

48. Roman Verostko, *East–West*, 2001, plotter drawing on paper, 29.5 × 37 cm

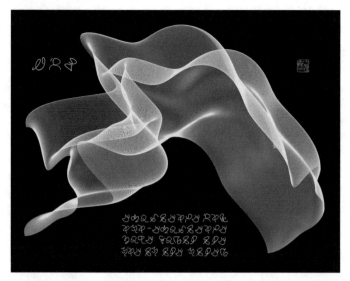

49. Roman Verostko, *San Marco Apocalypse: Lifting the Veil*, 2017, digital print, 55 × 30 cm

50. Roman Verostko, *Cosmic Immersion*, 1987, algorithmic pen and ink drawing, plotted drawing on paper, 60 × 45.7 cm

Further Reading

On the history of the Algorists: http://www.verostko.com/algorists.org.

Roman Verostko, Software As Genotype, A New Dimension of Art. Presented at the 1988 ISEA, it was then was published in *Leonardo*: *Leonardo*, Vol. 23, No. 1, 1990, pp. 17–23. Available online at http://verostko.com/epigenet.html.

Revisited version for *Ars Electronica, Genetic Art – Artificial Life*, 1993: http://verostko.com/arc hive/writings/notizen_zur_epigenetischen_kunst.htm.

Revisited again for *Ars Electronica, Code: The Language of Our Time*, 2003: http://verostko.com/archive/writings/epigen-art-revisited.html.

Chapter 7
Visual Documentation

The following sets of photographs aims at visually documenting Algorithmic Signs. They include gallery general shots and photographs taken in each room, each dedicated to one artist. As to the rooms captions, the curator chose to leave them to a minimum and to use quotes of the artists taken directly from the interviews she recorded with them to research her curatorial concept and in preparation for the exhibition, or from their writings.

The first set of six photographs (Figs. 7.1, 7.2, 7.3, 7.4, 7.5 and 7.6) shows the entrance of the Fondazione Bevilacqua La Masa Gallery in Saint Marks Square. The shape of this space inspired the author and curator to install a set of sculptural works by Manfred Mohr (P-499-Al, 1993) arranged in a way that they that create a sort of grid that welcomes the visitor to the exhibition, and two paintings by the same artist P1273_6351, 2008 and P1273_9168, from 2007.

The long corridor in front of the gallery entrance door—which is positioned under the loggia of St Marks Square, one of the most visited sites in the World, records a constant flow of passers-by throughout the day. This inspired the author and curator to commission Ernest Edmonds a site-specific installation, Growth and Form (2017), placed right in front of the gallery entrance door, that interacts with the movement of visitors entering the gallery.

Compared to the rest of the gallery space, organised in separate rooms, mostly squared, this particular space of the corridor that features original Renaissance column and marble floors, allowed more creativity in terms of curatorial choices and inspired the curator to play with the historical features of the building creating a lively contrast between old and new, introducing the visitor to the history of algorithmic art in a venue that has contributed to the development of contemporary art for over a century in one of the most iconic historical sites of the city.

© Springer Nature Switzerland AG 2022   149
F. Franco, *The Algorithmic Dimension*, Springer Series on Cultural Computing,
https://doi.org/10.1007/978-3-319-61167-9_7

Fig. 7.1 View of the gallery entrance. Manfred Mohr's installation P-499-Al, 1993

Fig. 7.2 View of the gallery entrance. Exhibition credits

Fig. 7.3 Entrance corridor view. Manfred Mohr's installation P-499-Al, 1993, and Ernest Edmonds' Growth and Form, 2017

Fig. 7.4 Entrance corridor view. Manfred Mohr's installation P-499-Al, 1993

Fig. 7.5 Entrance view. Ernest Edmonds' Growth and Form, 2017

Fig. 7.6 Entrance view. Manfred Mohr's P1273_6351, 2008 and P1273_9168, 2007

The following set of photographs (Figs. 7.7, 7.8, 7.9, 7.10, 7.11 and 7.12) shows the room dedicated to the work of Vera Molnar. The photographs capture a series of room general shots and a number of single artworks, sourced mostly from one of the most important and comprehensive private collections of computer art, the Anne and Michael Spalter Digital Art Collection. The works featuring in this room, selected with the artist, exemplify how Molnar's work starts from a series of seemingly simple concepts, like those shown on a series of plotter drawings in the vetrine (Vera Molnar, Untitled, 1974–1975, plotter drawings, pen), and develops in the most sophisticated way through a selection of gauche, collages, and computer-generated drawings. One of Molnar's most iconic work, inspired by Cèzanne's Mount St. Victoire (13 Variations Mount St. Victoire series, 1989–96, laserprint on paper, 31 × 43 cm each), has inspired the curator to realise, under the artist's instructions, a site-specific installation based on a single line made of black wool thread that traces the contours of Mount St. Victoire (Installation based on 13 Variations Mount St. Victoire series, nails and wool thread, 280 × 80 cm). The quote from Vera Molnar that welcomes the visitor to her room reads as follows:

Eseguite con computer e plotter, l'aspetto visivo di queste opere cambia in modo uniforme ad ogni riga, procedendo da sinistra a destra. Utilizzando un processo sempre più 'random', le linee - costruite attraverso una sequenza regolare di alti e bassi con un'angolazione di 110–120 gradi - diventano sempre più caotiche man mano che avanzano verso destra. Questo fenomeno si realizza di riga in riga e tra lettera e lettera. Le lettere diventano sempre più "disturbate" convulse. L'ordine relativo che appare nelle prime lettere, sulla sinistra, scompare progressivamente. Questa è una soluzione che fa rizzare i capelli a un'artista con una educazione classica come me, e suscita l'indignazione dei puristi. Non c'é simmetria, niente equilibrio, niente diagonali, niente triangoli nella composizione. L'unità del lavoro è assicurata unicamente dal fatto che si tratta di scrittura, e più esattamente di una simulazione di scrittura di mia madre. Questo fenomeno non rientra in alcuna categoria di composizione pittorica. Ciascuna di queste opere comprende rigore ed emozione, controllo e abbandono, ordine e follia. Nonostante l'intero processo sia contrario alle regole convenzionali, sono soddisfatta del risultato! (Molnar 1990)

The visual aspect in these pieces, executed with computer and plotter, changes evenly at every line, proceeding from left to right. Using an increasingly random process, the lines – built up with regular sequences going up and down with a tilt of 110–120 degrees – become more and more chaotic as they advance to the right. This phenomenon occurs within each line, within each letter. The letters become more and more disturbed. The relative order seen in the first letters, on the left side, disappears progressively. This is a hair-raising solution for a painter like myself with a classical education. There is no symmetry, no equilibrium, no transversal, no triangle. [...] I tried various ways to reconcile and bring together the two different and opposing areas: visual arts and my mother's dishevelled writing. Though the whole thing is against the rules, in practice I am pleased with the result! (Molnar 1990)

Fig. 7.7   View from Vera Molnar's room

Fig. 7.8   View from Vera Molnar's room

Fig. 7.9 View from Vera Molnar's room

Fig. 7.10 View from Vera Molnar's room

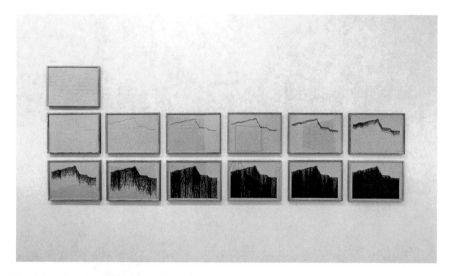

Fig. 7.11 View from Vera Molnar's room

Fig. 7.12 View from Vera Molnar's room

The following set of photographs (Figs. 7.13, 7.14, 7.15, 7.16, 7.17, 7.18, 7.19, 7.20 and 7.21) shows images taken from the room dedicated to the work of Manfred Mohr. The photographs capture a series of room general shots and a number of single artworks, sourced from Carroll/Fletcher gallery, London. The works featuring in this room, selected with the artist, exemplify the breath of Mohr's work that includes computer-generated algorithmic plotter drawings from the early 1970s and 1980s, paintings on canvas from the 1990s and early 2000s, and a series of screen-based generative animations that show a rotating diagonal-path of an n-dimensional hypercube and trace the history of n-dimensional rotations explored by Mohr in the 2010s. The works featured in this room aim to document Mohr's consistent creative force from the early 1970s until the mid-2010s.

Explaining the algorithm that generates some of the early plotter drawings featuring this room (P-021, 1970, plotter drawing on paper, 52 × 52 cm; P-036, 1970, plotter drawing on paper, 52 × 52 cm; plotter drawing on paper, 52 × 52 cm), Mohr says: "The elements are horizontal, vertical, 45 degree lines, square waves, zig-zags, and have probabilities for line widths and lengths. The algorithm places elements in a horizontal direction and has a high probability to move from left to right and a limited probability to backtrack. The original idea of this algorithm was to create a visual musical score which defies the progression in time by occasionally turning back on itself. Thus at the same time an abstract text is created."

The following is the quote used to introduce Mohr's room:

Chiamo la mia arte 'generativa' perché tutto il mio lavoro è generato da algoritmi (processi logici) ideati e programmati da me in precedenza. Questo è il mio principale contributo

Fig. 7.13 View from Manfred Mohr's room. Mohr's plotter drawing P-196-A, 1977

Fig. 7.14 View from Manfred Mohr's room. Mohr's plotter drawing P1622-G, 2012

Fig. 7.15 View from Manfred Mohr's room, with detail of his canvas P1011_D, 2004

Fig. 7.16   View from Manfred Mohr's room, with detail of his canvas *P1011_Ms*, 2004

alla ricerca estetica. Creo segni, esistenze grafiche, a partire da un contesto razionale. Questi segni riferiscono unicamente a se stessi e ciò che contengono è evidenza della loro creazione. L'introduzione del computer e del plotter nel 1969 hanno contribuito ad uno sviluppo logico e immediato della mia opera. Il dialogo con la macchina è diventato quindi una parte essenziale del mio lavoro – un'estensione irreversibile e un'amplificazione del mio pensiero artistico. (Mohr 1983)

I call my work 'generative' because all my work is generated from algorithms (logical processes) worked out by myself beforehand. This is my fundamental contribution to aesthetic research. I create signs, graphic existences, out of rational context. These signs refer only to themselves and their content is evidence of their creation. A logical and straight-forward development of my work was the introduction of a computer and of a plotter in 1969. Dialogue with the machine thus became an important part of my work - an irreversible extension and/or amplification of my artistic thought. (Mohr 1983)

Fig. 7.17 Manfred Mohr's P2210-C LCD, 2015 (left), and *P1680-C*, 2015 (right)

Fig. 7.18 View from Manfred Mohr's room

Fig. 7.19 View from Manfred Mohr's room

Fig. 7.20   View from Manfred Mohr's room

Fig. 7.21   View from Manfred Mohr's room

The following set of photographs (Figs. 7.22, 7.23, 7.24, 7.25 and 7.26) shows images taken from the room dedicated to the work of Frieder Nake. The photographs capture a series of room general shots and a number of single artworks, selected with the artist and sourced from the artist's personal archives and the Anne e Michael Spalter Digital Art Collection. They include a very early series of plotter inks on translucent paper from 1964, a series of early plotter drawings that were first exhibited in Venice during the 1970 Venice Biennale, a paper collage based on Nake's Matrix Multiplication series 40 from 1968, a serigraphy from the early 1970s and digital prints from the early 2000s and 2010s.

The quote from Frieder Nake that welcomes the visitor to his room reads as follows:

Matrix Multiplication, uno dei lavori di computer art più celebrati, torna a Venezia per la prima volta dopo l'esibizione alla Biennale del 1970. E'uno dei primi esempi di disegni realizzati completamente a colore continuo e generati dal computer. Consiste di una griglia nella quale ogni singolo tassello di colore viene assegnato da un processo matematico. Questo lavoro, come spiega Frank Dietrich nel 1986, "presenta una serie di variazioni che riflettono la traslazione da un processo puramente matematico a un processo estetico."

Matrix Multiplication, back in Venice since it was exhibited at the 1970 Biennale, represents one of the most iconic computer-generated artworks, and one of the earliest examples of full-colour continuous drawings generated by a computer. Consisting of a grid of little squares where colours have been assigned by mathematical process, the work presents a series of variations that, as Frank Dietrich described in 1986, "reflect the translation of a mathematical process into an aesthetic process."

Fig. 7.22 View from Frieder Nakes's room

Fig. 7.23 View from Frieder Nakes's room

Fig. 7.24 View from Frieder Nakes's room

Fig. 7.25 View from Frieder Nakes's room

Fig. 7.26 A view from Frieder Nakes's room

The following set of photographs (Figs. 7.27, 7.28, 7.29 and 7.30) shows images taken from the room dedicated to the work of Roman Verostko. The photographs capture a series of room general shots and a number of single artworks, selected with the artist and sourced from the Victoria and Albert Museum, the Anne e Michael Spalter Digital Art Collection, DAM Gallery Berlin and the artist's personal archives. They include a series of algorithmic pen and ink plotter drawings on paper from the mid-1980s, early 1990s and 2000s, a rare example of watercolour and crayon work on paper from Verostko's pre-computer phase in 1963, a printed text with computer-generated images from 1990, an eight-hour video documentary showing how one of Verostko's "Green Clouds" is generated using a pen plotter's drawing arm, and a new work specifically commissioned by the author and curator to Verostko, inspired by Venice and the St Mark's Apocalypse.

Fig. 7.27 View from Roman Verostko's room

Fig. 7.28 View from Roman Verostko's room

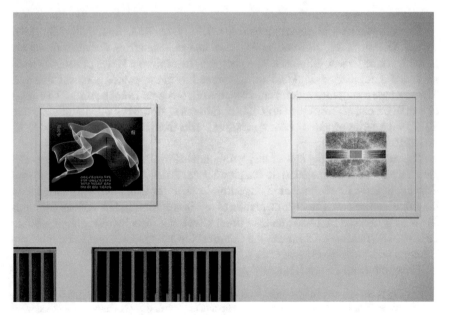

Fig. 7.29 View from Roman Verostko's room

Fig. 7.30 View from Roman Verostko's room

The following set of photographs (Figs. 7.31, 7.32, 7.33, 7.34, 7.35, 7.36, 7.37, 7.38, 7.39, 7.40, 7.41, 7.42 and 7.43) shows images taken from the room dedicated to the work of Ernest Edmonds. The photographs capture a series of room general shots and a number of single artworks, sourced from the artist's personal archives. They include a cellulose relief from 1975, a work on paper from the mid-1970s, a set of works on canvas from the early 1980s, Edmonds' first work on aluminium from 2017, and a series of video-based generative works from the mid-1990s, early 2000s and 2010s.

The extra space at the end of this room allowed the curator to install Edmonds' generative immersive installation, Shaping Space (2012). This is one of a number of Shaping Space's iterations that in Algorithmic Signs took an interesting turn due to the space limitations. The documentation of this installation and its various iterations has been published in a book chapter titled "Evolving Installations: Shaping Space 2012–2017", in Museums and Digital Culture: New Perspectives and Research, Tula Giannini and Jonathan Bowen (Eds.), Springer, 2019, 367–379.

The quote from Ernest Edmonds' room reads as follows:

Shaping Form consiste in una serie di schermi quadrati, originariamente delimitati da una cornice acrilica bianca. Ogni movimento che avviene davanti a ciascuno schermo viene percepito e catturato da una piccola videocamera. Questo porta a dei cambiamenti progressivi nel programma che genera le immagini. Un osservatore può notare la risposta immediata dell'opera al movimento ma, come Edmonds sottolinea, "i cambiamenti nel corso del tempo

Fig. 7.31 A detail from Ernest Edmonds' room with two Shaping Form screen-based works, 2015

Fig. 7.32 Detail from Ernest Edmonds' work. Fifty–Two, 1980

Fig. 7.33 Detail from Ernest Edmonds' work. *Fifty–Seven*, 1982–1984

Fig. 7.34 View from Ernest Edmonds' room

Fig. 7.35 View from Ernest Edmonds' room

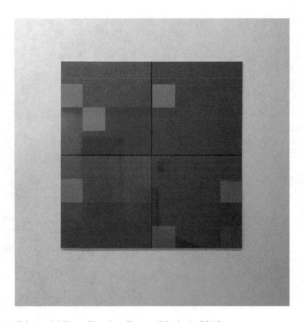

Fig. 7.36 Ernest Edmonds' Four Shaping Forms (Venice), 2015

Fig. 7.37 Detail from the first floor gallery. Ernest Edmonds' room

Fig. 7.38 Detail from the first floor gallery. Ernest Edmonds' immersive installation Shaping Space, 2012

Fig. 7.39 Detail of Ernest Edmonds' immersive installation Shaping Space, 2012

Fig. 7.40 Detail of Ernest Edmonds' immersive installation Shaping Space, 2012

Fig. 7.41   View of Ernest Edmonds' work. Shaping Space, 2012

Fig. 7.42   View of Ernest Edmonds' work. Shaping Form Series, 2007–15

Fig. 7.43 A view from Ernest Edmonds' room

si notano solamente nel caso di una visione più prolungata, anche se non necessariamente continuativa, dell'opera. Una prima visione seguita da una seconda nei mesi successivi rivelerà degli sviluppi chiaramente distinguibili sia nei colori che nella loro sequenza". (Edmonds 2007)

Shaping Form consists of a series of works on individual stand-alone screens framed so that the image is square. The early frames were in white acrylic. Movement in front of each work is detected by a small camera. This leads to continual changes in the program that generates the images. A viewer can readily detect the immediate responses of the work to movement but, as Edmonds points out, "the changes over time are only apparent when there is more prolonged, although not necessarily continuous, contact with it. A first viewing followed by one several months later will reveal noticeable developments in the colours and patterns." (Edmonds 2007)

The following set of images shows the floor plans of the Bevilacqua La Masa gallery (ground floor and first floor). Numbers in the map refer to the positioning of the artworks as they appeared in the *Algorithmic Signs* exhibition, while the numbered list below each map refers to the artwork labels. This arrangement is intended to reproduce the actual arrangement of the artworks in the exhibition. This numeration has been applied in the chapters of this book when a specific artwork is mentioned.

Ground Floor Plan

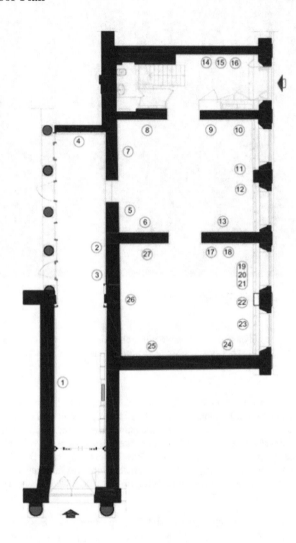

List of Artworks (Ground Floor)

1. Manfred Mohr, *P-499-Al*, 1993, painted steel, 15 parts, 250 × 1200 cm
2. Manfred Mohr, *P1273_6351*, 2008, pigments, ink on canvas, 90 × 90 cm
3. Manfred Mohr, *P1273_9168*, 2007, pigment ink on canvas, 90 × 90 cm
4. Ernest Edmonds, *Growth and Form*, 2017, Computer based interactive installation
5. Manfred Mohr, *P-196-A*, 1977, plotter drawing on paper, 50 × 50 cm
6. Manfred Mohr, *P1622-G*, 2012–14, LCD screen Mac Mini, 45 × 45 × 11 cm
7. Manfred Mohr, *P-231-C*, 1978, plotter drawing on paper, 51 × 82 cm
8. Manfred Mohr, *P-370-AZ*, 1984–85, plotter drawing, ink on paper, 65 × 92 cm
9. Manfred Mohr, *P2210-C LCD*, 2015, screen MacMini, 37 × 63 × 11 cm
10. Manfred Mohr, *P1680-C*, 2015, LCD screen MacMini, 37 × 63 × 11 cm
11. Manfred Mohr, *P1011_D*, 2004, pigment ink on canvas, 112 × 112 cm
12. Manfred Mohr, *P1011_Ms*, 2004, pigment ink on canvas, 112 × 11 cm
13. Manfred Mohr, *P-453-AK/2*, 1990, acrylic on canvas, 120 × 120 cm
14. Manfred Mohr, *P-021*, 1970, plotter drawing on paper, 52 × 52 cm
15. Manfred Mohr, *P-036*, 1970, plotter drawing on paper, 52 × 52 cm
16. Manfred Mohr, *P-122*, 1970, plotter drawing on paper, 52 × 52 cm
17. Vera Molnar, *Untitled*, 1974–1975, plotter drawings, pen
18. Vera Molnar, *Series Interruptions*, 1968, plotter drawing, 35 × 35 cm
19. Vera Molnar, *Lettres De Ma Mère*, 1983, plotter drawing, 29 × 25 cm
20. Vera Molnar, *Lettres De Ma Mère*, 1983, plotter drawing, 22 × 29 cm
21. Vera Molnar, *Lettres De Ma Mère*, 1983, plotter drawing, 20 × 36 cm
22. Vera Molnar, *Untitled*, 1983, plotter drawing, 32 × 33 cm
23. Vera Molnar, *Structure De Quadreilateres*, 1983, plotter drawing, 28 × 29 cm
24. Vera Molnar, *Installation based on 13 Variations Mount St. Victoire series*, nails and wool thread, 280 × 80 cm
25. Vera Molnar, *13 Variations Mount St. Victoire series*, 1989–96, laserprint on paper, 31 × 43 cm each
26. Vera Molnar, *144 Rectangles*, 1969, collage, 59 × 179 cm
27. Vera Molnar, *Untitled*, 1974, plotter drawing, 97 × 98 cm

First Floor Plan

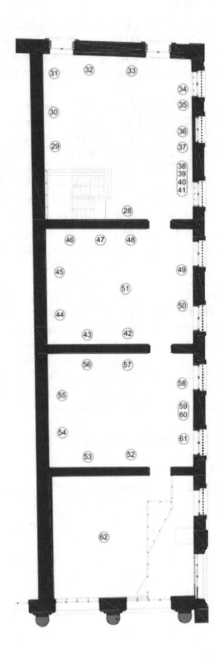

List of Artworks (First Floor)

28. Frieder Nake, *Walk through raster Montreal version*, 1972, screenprint
29. Frieder Nake, *Random polygons*, 1964, ink on transparent paper, 10 × 10 cm each
30. Frieder Nake, *12/7/65 Bundles of straight lines*, 1965, colored ink on paper, 82.5 × 67.2 cm
31. Frieder Nake, *Bundles of straight lines in grid*, 2015, digital print, 40 × 40 cm
32. Frieder Nake, *Generative Aesthetics I, Experiment 6.22*, 1968/69, cardboard tiles on fiberboard, 128 × 128 cm
33. Frieder Nake, *13/9/65 Nr. 2 "Homage to Paul Klee"*, 1965, ink on paper, 50 × 50 cm
34. Frieder Nake, *Matrix multiplication series 34*, 1968, colored ink on paper, 9 states, 40 × 40 cm
35. Frieder Nake, *Matrix multiplication series 40*, 1968, colored ink on paper, 4 states, 40 × 40 cm
36. Frieder Nake, *Nake/ER56/264*, 1969, plotter print, 21.7 × 16.7 cm
37. Frieder Nake, *25/2/65 Nr.14 random polygon, vertical–horizontal*, 1965, colored ink on paper, 4 colors, 42 × 55.5 cm
38. Frieder Nake, *Walk through raster Abteiberg version*, 2005, colored digital print, 40 × 40 cm
39. Frieder Nake, *Walk through raster Abteiberg version*, 2005, colored digital print, 40 × 40 cm
40. Frieder Nake, *Walk through raster Abteiberg version*, 2005, colored digital print, 40 × 40 cm
41. Frieder Nake, *Walk through raster Abteiberg version*, 2005, colored digital print, 40 × 40 cm
42. Roman Verostko, *Three Story Drawing Machine*, 2011, video documentation, approximately 8 h
43. Roman Verostko, *Untitled*, 1963, brush, watercolour and crayon, 73 × 93 cm
44. Roman Verostko, *Morning Song*, 2010, plotter drawing, pen and brush on paper, 76 × 56 cm
45. Roman Verostko, *Frog Jump*, 2010, plotter drawing, pen and brush on paper, 76 × 56 cm
46. Roman Verostko, *Sun Canticle*, 1996, algorithmic pen and ink drawing, plotted drawing on paper, 33 × 48 cm
47. Roman Verostko, *26 Visions of Hildegard*, 2001, plotter drawing on paper, 76 × 56 cm
48. Roman Verostko, *East–West*, 2001, plotter drawing on paper, 29.5 × 37 cm
49. Roman Verostko, *San Marco Apocalypse: Lifting the Veil*, 2017, digital print, 55 × 30 cm
50. Roman Verostko, *Cosmic Immersion*, 1987, algorithmic pen and ink drawing, plotted drawing on paper, 60 × 45.7 cm

51. Roman Verostko, *Derivations of the laws of the symbols of logic from the law of the operations of the human mind*, 1990, printed text and computer-generated images, 5.6 × 26 × 11 cm
52. Ernest Edmonds, *Fifty–Seven*, 1982–1984, acrylic on canvas, 122 × 122 cm
53. Ernest Edmonds, *Forty–Five*, 1975, cellulose relief, 60 × 60 cm
54. Ernest Edmonds, *Four Shaping Forms*, 2017, aluminium, 120 × 120 cm
55. Ernest Edmonds, *Fifty–Two*, 1980, acrylic on canvas 92 × 92 cm each
56. Ernest Edmonds, *Twenty–One*, 1976–1977, ink on paper, 56 × 56 cm
57. Ernest Edmonds, *Four Shaping Forms (Venice)*, 2015, aluminium
58. Ernest Edmonds, *Nagoya*, 1996, generative video
59. Ernest Edmonds, *Shaping Form*, 2015, generative interactive video
60. Ernest Edmonds, *Shaping Form*, 2015, generative interactive video
61. Ernest Edmonds, *Shaping Form*, 2007, generative interactive video, screen
62. Ernest Edmonds, *Shaping Space*, 2012, interactive installation

Printed in the United States
by Baker & Taylor Publisher Services